The Human Elements of Psychotherapy

The Human Elements of Psychotherapy

A Nonmedical Model of Emotional Healing

David N. Elkins

Foreword by Barry L. Duncan

American Psychological Association

Washington, DC

Published by
American Psychological Association
750 First Street, NE
Washington, DC 20002
www.apa.org

To order
APA Order Department
P.O. Box 92984
Washington, DC 20090-2984
Tel: (800) 374-2721; Direct: (202) 336-5510
Fax: (202) 336-5502; TDD/TTY: (202) 336-6123
Online: www.apa.org/pubs/books
E-mail: order@apa.org

In the U.K., Europe, Africa, and the Middle East, copies may be ordered from
American Psychological Association
3 Henrietta Street
Covent Garden, London
WC2E 8LU England

Typeset in Minion by Circle Graphics, Inc., Columbia, MD

Printer: Maple Press, York, PA
Cover Designer: Minker Design, Sarasota, FL

The opinions and statements published are the responsibility of the authors, and such opinions and statements do not necessarily represent the policies of the American Psychological Association.

Library of Congress Cataloging-in-Publication Data

Elkins, David N.
 The human elements of psychotherapy : a nonmedical model of emotional healing / David N. Elkins.
  pages cm
 Includes bibliographical references and index.
 ISBN 978-1-4338-2066-3 — ISBN 1-4338-2066-8 1. Psychotherapy. 2. Psychotherapy—Social aspects. I. Title.
 RC480.E43 2016
 616.89'14—dc23
                    2015011917

British Library Cataloguing-in-Publication Data
A CIP record is available from the British Library.

Printed in the United States of America
First Edition

http://dx.doi.org/10.1037/14751-000

To Sara, my best friend for more than 50 years

Contents

Foreword

Barry L. Duncan

Almost two years ago, David Elkins sent me a proposal for a book that he was planning to write. After reviewing the proposal, I wrote the following endorsement: "This is a book that has to be written! It uniquely combines relational sciences from diverse disciplines into a compelling whole that finally describes and defines psychotherapy by not only its participants but also the power inherent in human relationship and connection." Now that the book has been written, I am even more convinced that it will make an important contribution.

To my great delight, *The Human Elements of Psychotherapy* eviscerates the medical model using cogent scholarly, empirical, and logical arguments. Although the medical model, simplified to "diagnosis + prescriptive treatment = cure or symptom amelioration," is a valid way to approach physical problems, its assumptions do not hold up well in application to psychotherapy. It reduces clients to diagnoses and therapists to treatment technologies, or worse, it makes them irrelevant (Duncan & Reese, 2012). Just plug in the diagnosis, do the prescribed treatment, and voila, cure or symptom amelioration! This medical view of therapy is empirically vacuous because diagnosis yields little that is helpful and model/ technique accounts for so little of outcome variance, whereas the client and the therapist—and their relationship—account for so much more.

And yet, it remains the dominant paradigm in our field. Both insurance reimbursement and research funding depend on it. It gives a scientific aura and the illusion of clinical utility despite its deeply flawed assumptions.

The fact of the matter is that psychotherapy is decidedly a relational, not medical, endeavor (Duncan, 2014), one that is wholly dependent on the participants and the quality of their interpersonal connection. *The Human Elements of Psychotherapy* makes this abundantly clear and more.

There is so much to like about this unique book. Dr. Elkins provides not only the best critique of the medical model available but also a viable alternative based on the power of human relationships. One of the foundational ideas of *The Human Elements of Psychotherapy* is a focus on the participants of therapy and their relationship. The most potent factor of therapeutic change is the client, including his or her resources, resiliencies, and social contexts. Client factors account for up to 86% of outcome variance (derived from the oft-reported .80 effect size). Indeed, the client is the engine of change (Bohart & Tallman, 2010). In addition, recent investigations reveal that 5% to 8% of the overall variance is accounted for by the person of the therapist (Baldwin & Imel, 2013). Then there is that tried-and-true but taken for granted old friend, the therapeutic alliance. In a recent meta-analysis, Horvath, Del Re, Flückiger, and Symonds (2011) examined 201 studies and found the alliance to account for 7.5% of the variance. Given that model differences account for about 1% of the variance, and putting this into perspective, the amount of change attributable to the participants and their relationship far exceeds that of specific model or technique.

In *The Human Elements of Psychotherapy*, Dr. Elkins summarizes these findings but then goes beyond them to address the question: *Why* are the human elements so potent? To answer this question, he draws on evidence from the relationship sciences to show that humans are evolved to heal one another emotionally through social means. As Dr. Elkins puts it, "We are evolutionarily 'hard wired' to heal and be healed by human connection and social interaction. Thus, the human elements are the 'power center' for emotional healing in psychotherapy. Without those elements, psychotherapy could not heal." Although the idea that psychotherapy heals through "social means" is not new, this book covers new ground via a synthesis of evidence from numerous disciplines to construct a theoretical model of psychotherapy based on social healing. Using clinical evidence as the cornerstone, the book combines findings from attachment theory, social relationships research, neuroscience, and evolutionary theory to build a nonmedical model of psychotherapy that places the human elements at the center ... finally! In essence, the book provides an evidence-based theoretical structure of how emotional healing occurs and how psychotherapy works. To quote Dr. Elkins,

> We need to demystify psychotherapy and stop obfuscating its real nature by describing it in medical and technical terms. Psychotherapy, properly understood, is simply a relationship between a client who is in emotional pain and a therapist who is able and willing to help. This is not to equate psychotherapy with common, everyday relationships but, rather, to emphasize that psychotherapy is cut from the same cloth. Psychotherapy is effective because it draws on the power of human connection and social interaction to restore the client's emotional well-being. (p. 49)

Even two decades ago, mainstream clinical psychology would have considered this statement preposterous. Most clinicians and researchers thought (and many still do) that modalities and techniques were the agents of change and that relational factors were important only because they made clients more compliant with treatment. But times, as they say, are a-changing.

David Elkins was the ideal person to write this book. He is a fellow of the American Psychological Association (APA) and has served twice as president of Division 32, the Society for Humanistic Psychology, of APA. Dr. Elkins is a leading voice in humanistic–existential psychology; a professor emeritus of psychology in the Graduate School of Education and Psychology at Pepperdine University; an experienced clinician having worked in hospital, community mental health, and private-practice settings; and a noted author, having published many articles and two previous books. Thus, *The Human Elements of Psychotherapy* is rooted in Dr. Elkins's many years as a professor, clinician, and scholar. To say, however, that this renowned individual brings a world of experience, scholarship, insight, and humanity to life in the pages of this book would not do this book credit. This book offers much more than that. It guides the reader into introspection about the very foundation of our field as well as a continued reflection about what it means to be a psychotherapist. I am pleased to recommend it to clinicians, researchers, students, and others who are not satisfied with the medical paradigm and are interested in moving the field forward to an understanding of how healing occurs and how psychotherapy works.

In sum, this well-researched and provocative book offers a comprehensive critique of the misguided model that has for too long dominated our field and effortlessly escorts the reader into a consideration of psychotherapy from a different vantage point—a human one. This book reaffirmed my belief that the odds for change when you combine a resourceful client, a strong alliance, and an authentic therapist are worth betting on, certainly cause for hope, and responsible for my unswerving faith in psychotherapy as a healing endeavor. It's been a long time coming, and this book will help usher the way out of the medical model.

Acknowledgments

I owe a special debt of gratitude to Barry Duncan, director of the Heart and Soul of Change Project and one of the most influential clinicians of our time. Barry read and endorsed the original proposal for the book and graciously agreed to write the foreword.

I am also grateful to Irvin Yalom, Robert Stolorow, Gerald Corey, Arthur Bohart, Shawn Rubin, Thomas Greening, and Kirk Schneider, who also read and endorsed the original proposal. They are not responsible, of course, for any limitations of the completed book.

I thank Justin Underwood, my doctoral student at Pepperdine University, for locating publications, editing references, and performing other clerical tasks. Justin supported the project from the beginning and volunteered to do whatever he could to assist. More than words can express, I appreciate the many hours he gave to making this book a reality.

I also thank Drake Spaeth, associate professor of psychology at The Chicago School of Professional Psychology, and Shawn Rubin, editor-in-chief of the *Journal of Humanistic Psychology*, for reviewing the completed manuscript and making helpful suggestions. I am responsible, of course, for any limitations of the book.

I am also grateful to my graduate psychology students in the Graduate School of Education and Psychology at Pepperdine University. Many of the ideas in this book were first articulated and clarified in my classes and interactions with them.

I also thank Sara, my wife. As my "editor-in-residence," she made sure that the book was written in an accessible style. Sara believes scholarly writing is often unnecessarily obscure, so she insists that I write in a way that can actually be understood!

Finally, I thank my editors and the publishing staff at the American Psychological Association. I am especially grateful to Susan Reynolds, senior acquisitions editor, and Beth Hatch, the development editor for my book. Susan provided guidance at the proposal stage, and Beth edited the completed manuscript, providing expert guidance that made the book much stronger.

The Human Elements
of Psychotherapy

Introduction

Increasing evidence shows that common factors, and particularly human factors (e.g., client factors, therapist factors, the therapeutic alliance), are the primary determinants of effectiveness in psychotherapy, dwarfing the effects of modalities and techniques. This evidence undermines the medical model of psychotherapy with its assumption that modalities and techniques are the instruments of change and calls for a new, nonmedical model that places the human elements at the center of therapeutic work.

I did not begin my professional career believing that the human elements of psychotherapy were the primary determinants of effectiveness. As a graduate student in clinical psychology in the 1970s, I was taught that the human elements of psychotherapy were important because they helped build a good therapeutic relationship that, in turn,

http://dx.doi.org/10.1037/14751-001
The Human Elements of Psychotherapy: A Nonmedical Model of Emotional Healing, by D. N. Elkins

made the client more cooperative and compliant with the treatment. The "treatment" was the techniques and procedures used by the therapist. However, as I gained clinical experience as a young psychologist, I began to notice that when I had a good relationship with a client, he or she tended to get better, and I wasn't convinced that the change was due to the techniques I used. I was also aware that Carl Rogers's research in the 1950s and 1960s had shown that personal and interpersonal factors such as empathy, unconditional positive regard, and congruence were responsible for therapeutic change. Thus, I began to suspect that the human elements of therapy were the primary factors in emotional healing.

However, about this time in my career, proponents of cognitive–behavior therapy (CBT) began to publish articles and books indicating that certain CBT techniques had been scientifically proven to be effective for various disorders. By this time, I had begun to train therapists as a full-time professor at Pepperdine University. Excited about the "scientifically validated" techniques of CBT, I invited a leading CBT clinician to speak to one of my graduate classes. The students and I were very impressed. Like many clinicians during that era, I thought that CBT techniques were the royal road to scientific effectiveness. I continued to believe that the human elements of therapy were important but became convinced, once again, that the real agents of change were scientifically validated techniques.

Then, during the late 1990s and early 2000s, something happened that changed my understanding of how psychotherapy works. Bruce Wampold, a professor at the University of Wisconsin–Madison, published what would become landmark studies on psychotherapy effectiveness (Ahn & Wampold, 2001; Messer & Wampold, 2002; Waehler, Kalodner, Wampold, & Lichtenberg, 2000; Wampold, 2001a; Wampold et al., 1997). Wampold conducted analyses and meta-analyses of hundreds of published studies to identify the factors that were responsible for therapeutic effectiveness. Remarkably, the findings showed that techniques had little to do with effectiveness and that common factors were the real agents of change. Subsequent research confirmed these original findings (see, e.g., Benish, Imel, & Wampold, 2008; Imel, Wampold, Miller, & Fleming, 2008; Miller, Wampold, & Varhely, 2008). This evidence had a major impact on my understanding of psychotherapy and how it works. It also had a major impact on our profession. In fact, it shook, and continues to shake, the foundations of clinical psychology. The evidence showed that the medical model was wrong and that for more than a century, clinical research, training, and practice had focused on the wrong factors in psychotherapy.

Today, we are in the midst of a paradigmatic shift that is moving our profession toward a new understanding of emotional healing and a new understanding of how psychotherapy works. In essence, that's what this book is about. It presents a new, nonmedical model that places the human elements at the center of therapeutic work. But before delving into this new model, we need to examine its precursor, the medical model.

DEFINITION OF THE MEDICAL MODEL

The term *medical model of psychotherapy* can be confusing. For example, some clinicians think the term refers only to the neurobiological model and the use of psychiatric drugs. Because these clinicians use "talk therapy" to help clients, they think the medical model has nothing to do with them. Thus, it's important to emphasize that the term *medical model of psychotherapy* refers to any therapeutic approach, including talk therapy, that focuses on modalities and techniques and uses a medical schema and medical language to describe what is taking place. Elsewhere (Elkins, 2009a) I defined the medical model as follows:

> The medical model in psychotherapy is a descriptive schema borrowed from the practice of medicine and superimposed on the practice of psychotherapy. The schema, including its assumptions and language, accurately describes the processes and procedures of medical practice and has been highly useful in that field. However, the schema does not accurately describe the processes and procedures of psychotherapy and has proven itself to be problematic when superimposed on that field. In medicine, a doctor diagnoses a patient on the basis of symptoms and administers treatment designed to cure the patient's illness. In psychotherapy, medical model adherents *say* that a doctor diagnoses a patient on the basis of symptoms and administers treatment designed to cure

the patient's illness. However, when they say this, they are superimposing a medical schema on psychotherapy and using medical terms to describe what is essentially an interpersonal process that has almost nothing to do with medicine. (p. 40)

In other words, the medical model is a template or mold that Freud and other pioneers borrowed from medicine and superimposed on psychotherapy, forcing the language, processes, and procedures of psychotherapy into a medical-like pattern. Unfortunately, succeeding generations of clinicians also embraced the medical model. Thus, psychotherapy never had a chance to reveal its own natural or indigenous character. Today, we have become so accustomed to viewing psychotherapy through the lens of the medical model that it's difficult to see psychotherapy as it really is.

WHAT PSYCHOTHERAPY REALLY IS

When we examine the medical model from a clinical perspective, one of the first things we notice is that a typical psychotherapy session has almost nothing to do with medicine. A typical session consists of a client with some type of personal or interpersonal problem talking to a therapist who listens, offers support, and may suggest some ideas or an approach to the problem that might help. There is nothing about the process, if viewed objectively, that would lead one to describe it in medical terms. Of course, we can force the process into the medical model mold and then say that a "doctor" is "administering treatment" to a "patient." Such a description, however, seems forced and alien to what is actually taking place. If we describe what is happening without first forcing it into the mold of the medical model, it's really quite simple: Two people are talking; one is talking about a problem, and the other is listening and trying to help. There's no reason to distort what is taking place by forcing it into a mold borrowed from medicine. Psychotherapy has its own character. It's a social interaction, an interpersonal process. Surely, even ardent supporters of the medical model can see that it requires a stretch in logic, not to mention a certain lack of sensitivity, to say that listening to a woman pour out her grief about the loss of a child and offering support is a medical treatment or that trying to comfort an old man talking about his abject loneliness since his wife died is a medical procedure. Yet, these are the kinds of real-life issues that psychotherapists deal with every day.

Those of us who practice psychotherapy have the privilege of being invited into the most private chambers of our clients' lives. If we remove our medical model glasses, it's easy to see that psychotherapy is not a medical procedure. Instead, it's a special kind of relationship between a client who is having a difficult time and a therapist who is trying to help. The medical model has no language to describe these human and relational aspects of psychotherapy. Indeed, the medical model is a cold, insensitive system that distorts and obscures what is a deeply human, interpersonal process. Thus, even before we consider the scientific evidence that undermines the medical model, it's obvious that the model is problematic and that we need a new model of psychotherapy—one that reflects the true nature of psychotherapy and one whose language is not so cold and insensitive to the emotional pain and struggles of our clients.

WHY THE MEDICAL MODEL DOMINATES THE FIELD

If the medical model of psychotherapy is so problematic, then why does it continue to dominate our field? To answer this question, we must examine the politics and economics of the medical model.

Politics

I use the term *politics* here to refer to the dynamics of power associated with the medical model. First, most of the power structures associated with contemporary psychotherapy are permeated by the medical model. These power structures include psychology associations, training programs, research centers, research funding agencies, health insurance organizations, hospitals, mental health centers, and even private practice settings. These organizations are deeply rooted in the medical model, and if they abandoned that model and adopted a nonmedical model, they would have to make radical changes. In fact, they would have to change almost everything they have assumed about psychotherapy and how it works.

Second, the medical model provides a type of status and prestige for psychotherapy because of the model's association with two powerful systems in our culture: medicine and science. When we use terms such as *doctor, patient, symptoms, diagnosis, illness,* and *treatment,* we align psychotherapy with medicine, the most respected and powerful system of healing in Western culture. Similarly, when we use such terms as *scientifically validated techniques* or *empirically supported treatments,* we align psychotherapy with science, the most respected and powerful epistemological system in our culture. Thus, when psychotherapy is described in medical and scientific terms, it takes on an aura of prestige and power borrowed from medicine and science. Imagine the loss of prestige and power that would occur if we described psychotherapy as "listening to a person who is demoralized, experiencing emotional pain, or having other difficulties in life and giving that person support and guidance based on our experience and psychological knowledge." Although this description is quite accurate in terms of what most of us actually do, it lacks the connotations of prestige and power that are associated with saying that we are "doctors who diagnose psychopathology and administer empirically supported treatments to cure mental disorders." The first description conjures up images of a teacher, pastor, counselor, or even a caring friend who is helping another human being who is having a difficult time. The second description conjures up images of physician-like experts administering medical treatments that are scientifically proven to cure mental disorders. The power and prestige differential in these two descriptive systems is obvious. The first description suggests that psychotherapy is a special kind of relationship and human interaction. The second suggests that psychotherapy is a medical procedure that has all the power and credibility of medicine and science. Add to this the fact that health insurance companies are willing to pay "doctors" for "treating" "mental disorders" but are not willing to pay someone, even a professional with years of training and clinical experience, to listen to a demoralized person and offer support and guidance, and one can see why the medical model is so entrenched in our profession. To put it simply, the medical model remains the dominant descriptive system in psychotherapy not because it offers the most accurate description of what actually occurs in psychotherapy but, rather, because the model gives psychotherapy a level of prestige and power that other descriptive systems do not.

Economics

Another reason the medical model remains dominant is money. The economic well-being of thousands of clinicians, researchers, professors, administrators, and others is intertwined with the medical model. The same is true with hundreds of psychology-related organizations, as noted previously. To change the model could have a negative financial impact on these professionals and organizations.

Fortunately, our profession is based on science, not on power and money, so evidence must be the ultimate criterion by which we decide the future directions of our field. However, because of the political and economic forces that hold the medical model in place, the transition to a nonmedical model will not be easy. As Duncan, Miller, Wampold, and Hubble (2010) wrote,

> The medical model for psychotherapy remains robust, and its reach into every aspect of clinical work is deep. To move beyond it, to accept and then put to use the latest science, will require nothing short of a paradigmatic shift. (p. 428)

PURPOSE AND ORGANIZATION OF THE BOOK

Because the evidence undermining the medical model of psychotherapy is now so compelling, this may be the best time in the history of psychotherapy to replace it. Thus, at a practical level, the purpose of this book is to show that the medical model has been scientifically discredited and to present an alternative model that is aligned with the findings of science. However, at a deeper level, the purpose of the book is to provide a new understanding of emotional healing and thus a new understanding of psychotherapy. These two purposes converge as they are fleshed out in the following chapters.

The organization of the book is straightforward. Drawing on evidence from clinical psychology, attachment theory, social relationships research, neuroscience, evolutionary theory, and history, the first four chapters present a new understanding of emotional healing and lay foundations for a new model of psychotherapy. Chapter 1 summarizes evidence from clinical research to show that common factors, and particularly human factors, are the most potent determinants of effectiveness in psychotherapy. Chapter 2 describes evidence from attachment theory and social relationships research to show that we are evolved to develop, maintain, and restore our emotional well-being through supportive relationships with others and that psychotherapy is an expression of that evolutionarily derived ability. Chapter 3 presents findings from neuroscience and evolutionary theory to show that our brains evolved in a social context with remarkable abilities, including the ability to change in response to social experience and the ability to give and receive emotional healing through social means. The chapter shows how psychotherapy draws on these abilities to heal the client. Chapter 4 describes moral treatment as a historical example of an approach that used social means to heal those with severe psychological problems. Building on the scientific and historical foundations laid in the first four chapters, Chapter 5 presents a summary of the nonmedical model of psychotherapy and discusses the implications of the model for clinical research, training, and practice. The book concludes with a brief afterword.

I hope the book contributes to the growing realization among clinicians and researchers that the real power of emotional healing lies not in medical-like techniques but, rather, in the human elements of psychotherapy.

1

Clinical Psychology: Clinical Evidence for a Nonmedical Model

The medical model of psychotherapy, with its emphasis on modalities and techniques, has dominated the field for more than a century, from the time of Freud to the present (Bohart & Tallman, 1996, 1999, 2010; Elkins, 2009a, 2009b; Wampold, 2001a, 2001b). Today, the medical model is embraced by the health insurance industry, the American Psychiatric Association, the Association for Psychological Science, and the National Institute of Mental Health, and even by members of the U.S. Congress when they discuss national health care. Terms such as *doctor, patient, symptoms, diagnosis, mental disorders,* and *treatment* are the language currency of the "mental health" field.

Despite the dominance of the medical model, increasing numbers of clinicians and researchers are realizing that it is scientifically problematic (e.g., Bergin & Lambert, 1978; Bohart & Tallman, 1996, 1999; Duncan, Miller, Wampold, & Hubble, 2010; Elkins, 2009a, 2009b, 2012a, 2012b;

http://dx.doi.org/10.1037/14751-002
The Human Elements of Psychotherapy: A Nonmedical Model of Emotional Healing, by D. N. Elkins

Wampold, 2001a, 2010). From an evidence perspective, the weakest feature of the medical model is its assumption that modalities and techniques are the instruments of change. This assumption, which shapes clinical research, training, and practice, is a foundational component of the model. If the assumption is wrong, then the medical model must be dismantled and replaced by a new model of emotional healing that reflects the findings of science.

As this chapter will show, compelling evidence now makes it clear that modalities and techniques have relatively little to do with therapeutic change and that common factors, and particularly human factors, are the major determinants of effectiveness in psychotherapy. This chapter suggests that the evidence has now reached "critical mass" and that it's time for the field of psychotherapy to make a paradigmatic shift away from the medical model to bring clinical research, training, and practice into alignment with the findings of contemporary science.

THE SHADOW CULTURE AND SIGNS OF CHANGE

Although the medical model has always dominated clinical psychology, for the past 75 years or so there has been a "shadow culture" of researchers and clinicians who believed that common factors, not specific modalities and techniques, are the primary determinants of effectiveness in psychotherapy (e.g., Alarcon & Frank, 2012; Bergin & Lambert, 1978; Duncan et al., 2010; Elkins, 2007; Frank & Frank, 1991; Lambert & Barley, 2002; Lambert & Bergin, 1994; Lipsey & Wilson, 1993; Luborsky, Singer, & Luborsky, 1975; Orlinsky, Grave, & Parks, 1994; Orlinsky, Ronnestad, & Willutzki, 2004; Rachman & Wilson, 1980; Robinson, Berman, & Neimeyer, 1990; C. Rogers, 1957; Rosenzweig, 1936; Shadish, Navarro, Matt, & Phillips, 2000; Shapiro & Shapiro, 1982; M. L. Smith & Glass, 1977; M. L. Smith, Glass, & Miller, 1980; Wampold, 2001a). In recent years, this shadow culture has had a major impact on mainstream thinking. As a result, increasing numbers of clinicians and researchers are realizing that modalities and techniques have relatively little to do with effectiveness, whereas common factors are potent determinants of change. Thus, what was once a shadow culture is slowly becoming mainstream culture.

The signs of change can be seen in many places. For example, in 1999, Hubble, Duncan, and Miller published *The Heart and Soul of Change*, a book that emphasized the importance of common factors in psychotherapy. The book, published by the American Psychological Association (APA), had a significant effect on mainstream clinical thinking. In 2010, the second edition was published with updated research information and with Bruce Wampold as the fourth editor. Following publication of the original edition, Wampold had conducted extensive research on psychotherapy effectiveness, which showed that common factors, not modalities and techniques, were the primary agents of change. Thus, the first and second editions of *The Heart and Soul of Change*, along with Wampold's research findings, have had a major impact on mainstream clinical thinking. In the preface to the second edition, the editors wrote,

> Despite the field's love affair with technique, nearly a half century of empirical investigation has revealed that the effectiveness of psychotherapy resides not in the many variables that ostensibly distinguish one approach from another. Instead, the success of treatment is principally found in the factors that all approaches share in common. (Duncan et al., 2010, p. xxvii)

As another sign of change, in 2012, *The British Journal of Psychiatry* published an article authored by 29 psychiatrists that called for changes in the current paradigm of psychiatry, which emphasizes biomedical and technical procedures (see Bracken et al., 2012). The authors urged psychiatry to place more emphasis on clinical contact and interactions with patients. To show why this paradigm change is needed, they referred to the evidence that undermines techniques and supports common factors as the agents of change. They wrote, "The evidence that non-specific factors, as opposed to specific techniques, account for nearly all the change in therapy is overwhelming" (p. 431).

Yet another sign of change is that in 2013, Cromby, Harper, and Reavey published *Psychology, Mental Health and Distress*, a textbook aimed at undergraduate and graduate students in psychology. The book, which is based on the latest research, was written as an alternative to the typical "abnormal psychology" textbooks that emphasize biological causality and are organized around psychiatric categories of "psychopathology." Although it includes biological perspectives, *Psychology, Mental Health and Distress* emphasizes the role of relational and societal factors in the causation and amelioration of psychological problems. As the first mainstream textbook to take this broader, more sophisticated approach, the book reflects a growing realization among psychologists and other clinicians that the medical model has serious limitations. The book has been adopted by numerous programs in the United Kingdom and internationally. As an indication of the book's quality and groundbreaking importance, it won the 2014 British Psychological Society's textbook award.

Also, in a recent book dedicated to the legacy of Jerome Frank (Alarcon & Frank, 2012), the editors wrote that Frank's views on common factors "have become so widely accepted that they do not require extensive discussion" (p. xviii). For 50 years, Frank conducted research at Johns Hopkins University on psychotherapy's effectiveness. He was the first clinical scientist to conduct extensive and rigorous research on the question of what factors in psychotherapy account for its effectiveness. His findings consistently showed that common factors, not specific modalities and techniques, were the primary agents of change. In 1961, Frank published *Persuasion and Healing: A Comparative Study of Psychotherapy*, a book that summarized his research and made the bold suggestion that psychotherapy's effectiveness was due to common factors, not to specific modalities and techniques. Despite the fact it challenged almost everything mainstream clinical psychology believed about psychotherapy, the book was widely read and went through two additional editions (Frank's work is discussed in this chapter).

Perhaps the most dramatic sign of change is that in August 2012, the APA Council of Representatives, the policymaking body of APA, voted to adopt a Resolution on the Recognition of Psychotherapy Effectiveness (see http://www.apa.org/about/policy/resolution-psychotherapy.aspx). The resolution was designed to underscore the effectiveness of psychotherapy. Although it does not explicitly challenge the medical model, the resolution does mention that a variety of psychotherapies are effective and that the therapeutic relationship is an important factor in effectiveness. In addition, the resolution refers to the research of Bruce Wampold, whose analyses and meta-analyses of hundreds of published studies showed that common factors, not specific modalities and techniques, are the primary agents of change in psychotherapy (see a description of Wampold's contributions below in this chapter). The resolution also mentions the work of John Norcross (2001, 2002), who documented the extensive evidence that the client–therapist relationship is a major factor in therapeutic effectiveness. The "Resolution on the Recognition of Psychotherapy Effectiveness," which represents the official position of APA (2012), is important because APA, with a membership of almost 130,000, is the largest and most influential psychology association in the world.

Other signs of change could be noted, but perhaps the previously mentioned are sufficient to show that the shadow culture is slowly becoming mainstream. Our profession is realizing that the medical model has been undermined by the compelling evidence that common factors, and particularly human factors, are the most potent determinants of effectiveness in psychotherapy. The following two sections summarize this evidence.

EVIDENCE FOR COMMON FACTORS

This section summarizes evidence showing that common factors are the most potent elements in emotional healing. The section describes individuals who have made major contributions to the common factors perspective, along with their specific contributions.

Saul Rosenzweig

In 1936, Saul Rosenzweig published a short four-page journal article with the title "Some Implicit Common Factors in Diverse Methods of Psychotherapy" and an opening phrase from Lewis Carroll that reads "At last the Dodo said, '*Everybody* has won and *all* must have prizes.'"

Rosenzweig was the first person in history to publish an article suggesting that common factors might be responsible for psychotherapy's effectiveness. His article addressed a conundrum: How is it possible that diverse psychotherapies can all point to examples of therapeutic success?

In other words, if specific modalities and techniques are responsible for effectiveness, why is it that diverse therapies, which differ widely in modalities and techniques, are all effective? Rosenzweig's answer was that diverse psychotherapies are effective because of common factors found in all therapy systems. The reference to the Dodo bird in the opening phrase of Rosenzweig's article is from *Alice in Wonderland*. The Dodo was judging a race, but after the race, he couldn't decide who had won. So he finally declared, "Everyone has won and all must have prizes." Rosenzweig's point, of course, was that all psychotherapies have "won" because they are all effective. Today, when researchers mention the "Dodo bird verdict," they are referring to Rosenzweig's hypothesis that effectiveness in diverse therapies is due to common factors.

In 2000, Barry Duncan found Saul Rosenzweig still alive and living in St. Louis, Missouri (Rosenzweig died in 2004 at the age of 97). Duncan visited Rosenzweig and interviewed him about his 1936 article and other topics. The interview was published in *The Heart and Soul of Change* (second edition; see Duncan, 2010a), along with a reprint of Rosenzweig's 1936 article. Rosenzweig, who was in his early 90s at the time of the interview, displayed a generosity of spirit and a wonderful sense of humor. He was still convinced that common factors were responsible for the effectiveness of diverse therapies. When Duncan told him that it was still controversial, even today, to challenge the validity of specific therapies, Rosenzweig laughingly replied, "Not surprising, really. Psychotherapy models and their followers are more like cults: charismatic leaders with legions of worshippers" (Duncan, 2010a, p. 16).

George Kelly

George Kelly had a significant influence on American psychology. In 1946, he became director of training at Ohio State University. For 20 years, he trained clinicians and developed a strong research program in the psychology department. In 1955, Kelly published his magnum opus, *The Psychology of Personal Constructs*. The book foreshadowed the current interest in postmodernism and social constructivism.

Kelly is not usually included in discussions about common factors, but he made a discovery in the 1930s that should not be ignored. During the Great Depression, Kelly worked with poor, uneducated farmers in western Kansas, which was part of the Dust Bowl. After receiving his doctorate in psychology from the State University of Iowa in 1931, Kelly began teaching at Kansas State College in Fort Hays. In addition to teaching, he decided to offer counseling services to the people of the region. Although he had rejected psychoanalysis when he was a student, it was the only counseling approach he knew, so he asked his clients to lie on a couch, free associate, tell their dreams, and talk about their problems. Kelly then did his best to make "interpretations" based on his limited knowledge of Freudian theory. To his surprise, these uneducated farmers readily accepted his interpretations and made positive changes in their lives. Despite his therapeutic success, however, Kelly continued to doubt that the Freudian content of his interpretations was responsible for his clients' improvement. So he decided to try an experiment. Kelly (1963) said,

> I began fabricating "insights." I deliberately offered "preposterous interpretations" to my clients. Some of them were about as un-Freudian as I could make them. . . . My only criteria were that the explanation account for the crucial facts as the client saw them, and that it carry implications for approaching the future in a different way. (p. 52)

As Kelly had suspected, the fabricated "insights" and "preposterous interpretations" were just as effective as the ones based on Freudian theory. Clients accepted the explanations and made changes in their lives. Kelly concluded that it didn't matter whether an interpretation was based on Freudian theory or fabricated. What mattered was that the interpretation made sense to the client and carried implications for change.

Kelly's discovery, made more than 75 years ago, is in line with contemporary evidence that one's theory and techniques have relatively little to do with effectiveness and that other factors in the therapeutic situation are primarily responsible for client change.

Carl Rogers

Carl Rogers, one of the founders of humanistic psychology, was the first person in history to conduct major studies on psychotherapy using quantitative methods (Bozarth, Zimring, & Tausch, 2001). For nearly 20 years, Rogers and his associates at the University of Chicago conducted research focused on identifying the ingredients in psychotherapy that are responsible for therapeutic change. Rogers's findings consistently showed that personal and interpersonal factors, not medical-like techniques, were the ingredients of effectiveness. In 1957, Rogers published a major article on what he called "the necessary and sufficient conditions" for therapeutic change. The article identified three major conditions having to do with the therapeutic process itself: unconditional positive regard, empathic understanding of the client's internal frame of reference, and therapist congruence (i.e., genuineness). Of course, Rogers knew that no therapist can be "perfectly" caring, empathic, and congruent at all times, but his research indicated that *to the degree* these conditions are present, the client will tend to move in positive therapeutic directions. Although Rogers was trained in the medical model, he rejected that model early in his career in favor of what he called a *nondirective* approach that focused on helping clients clarify their thoughts and feelings. In time, Rogers changed the name of his approach to *client-centered therapy* and later to *person-centered approach.*

For his contributions to the field, APA gave Rogers the Award for Distinguished Scientific Contributions in 1956 and the Award for Distinguished Professional Contributions to Psychology in 1972. Rogers was the first psychologist in history to receive both awards (Cain & Seeman, 2002). In 1982, in a survey conducted by the *American Psychologist* (see D. Smith, 1982), Rogers was named the most influential psychotherapist and in 2007, in a survey conducted by *Psychotherapy Networker* ("The Top Ten," 2007), Rogers was again ranked number one. In 1987, Rogers was nominated for the Nobel Peace Prize for his efforts to bring rival factions together in Northern Ireland and South Africa.

I mention Rogers's accomplishments to show how difficult it is to dislodge the medical model. Even Carl Rogers, one of the most influential researchers and clinicians in history, was unable to persuade our profession to adopt a nonmedical approach to psychotherapy. In fact, despite Rogers's influence and his consistent findings that therapeutic change is due to personal and interpersonal factors, clinical researchers made a radical 180-degree turn away from Rogers's findings to specificity research in the 1970s. The term *specificity research* refers to the search for specific techniques to cure specific disorders, similar to the way medical scientists search for specific drugs to cure specific physical disorders. It's not clear why this 180-degree turn occurred, but from the 1970s to the end of the century, clinical scientists went in search of "silver bullet" techniques that could heal specific disorders. They conducted hundreds of efficacy studies in efforts to demonstrate that a particular modality or technique was more effective than other modalities and techniques. This was done despite the fact that in the 1970s, Luborsky, Singer, and Luborsky (1975) and M. L. Smith and Glass (1977) showed that all bona fide psychotherapies, despite differences in modalities and techniques, were effective. This should have alerted specificity researchers to the possibility that factors other than modalities and techniques might be responsible for psychotherapy's effectiveness. However, just as specificity researchers had ignored Rogers's findings, they also ignored these findings and forged ahead in search of specific techniques to cure specific disorders. During the 1980s and 1990s, dozens of articles appeared in major journals describing the special effectiveness of this or that modality or technique. For a while, it seemed that specificity research was paying off and that, indeed, powerful techniques had been developed to vanquish specific disorders. This was the heyday of cognitive–behavior therapy (CBT) and its proponents who insisted that they had developed specific techniques for specific disorders that were scientifically proven to be more effective than other techniques. Now, of course, all of those studies are in question because of analyses and meta-analyses conducted over the last 15 years or so that showed that the techniques described in the articles were not really responsible for the healing that occurred. In fact, after 40 years of specificity research, hundreds of efficacy studies, and millions of research dollars, there is still no scientific basis for privileging one modality or set of techniques over any other modality or set of techniques (Duncan et al., 2010; Elkins, 2009a; Wampold, 2001a). Thus, it seems that Rogers was right to reject the medical model and insist that personal and interpersonal factors are the effective ingredients in psychotherapy. (For more information on the contributions of Rogers, along with information on the political and economic forces with which Rogers had to contend when he opposed the medical model, see Bohart & Greening, 2001; Bozarth, Zimring, & Tausch, 2001; Cain & Seeman, 2002; Elkins, 2009b; Kirschenbaum, 2009; Kirschenbaum & Jourdan, 2005; C. Rogers, 1951, 1957, 1959, 1977; C. Rogers & Dymond, 1954; N. Rogers, 2008).

Lester Luborsky, Barton Singer, and Lise Luborsky

In 1975, Luborsky, Singer, and Luborsky published an article describing their review of 40 studies in which various psychotherapies had been used. The findings showed that all the psychotherapies were effective, even though they differed in modalities and techniques. This article had a significant impact on the profession. It was important not only because it affirmed that all therapies are effective but also because the article represented a change from focusing on individual studies to analyzing a large number of studies to arrive at a more valid conclusion. The article set the stage for the more sophisticated meta-analysis of 375 studies that M. L. Smith and Glass (1977) published 2 years later.

Mary Smith and Gene Glass

In 1977, Mary Smith and Gene Glass published an article in the *American Psychologist* titled "Meta-Analysis of Psychotherapy Outcome Studies." This was the first time that meta-analytic techniques had been used to analyze research studies on psychotherapy effectiveness. M. L. Smith and Glass analyzed 375 studies and found that psychotherapy was robustly effective and that all psychotherapies worked about equally well. The meta-analysis was criticized for methodological reasons, so in 1982, Landman and Dawes (1982) reanalyzed the 375 studies plus 60 of their own and still found that all psychotherapies, despite differences in modalities and techniques, were effective. The meta-analysis by M. L. Smith and Glass is now considered one of the turning points in the debate about whether psychotherapy is effective. M. L. Smith and Glass's study, along with the reanalysis by Landman and Dawes, helped silence those who had insisted that psychotherapy was not effective. Indeed, we now know that roughly 80% of those who go to therapy will be better off than those who don't, and some of them will be a great deal better off (Duncan et al., 2010; Lambert, 1986; Wampold, 2001a). Equally important, M. L. Smith and Glass's study also showed that all psychotherapies worked about equally well, suggesting that common factors, not specific modalities and techniques, are the primary determinants of effectiveness.

Hans Strupp and Suzanne Hadley

In 1979, Hans Strupp and Suzanne Hadley conducted an experiment in which they placed college students needing psychotherapy with either professional therapists or professors who had a reputation for being warm and trustworthy. The professional therapists had an average of 20 years of experience conducting therapy. The professors, who were professors of English, history, mathematics, or philosophy, had no training or experience conducting therapy. The findings were striking: Students in both groups improved, and there were no differences in effectiveness between the two "therapies." Strupp and Hadley (1979) suggested that the positive changes in both groups were due to the healing effects of a relationship with a benign human being. These findings support one of the major themes of this book: Humans are evolved to give and receive emotional healing through social means. As a result, any warm, caring human being can have a positive effect on the emotional well-being of another.

Jerome Frank

For 50 years, Jerome Frank, a professor of psychiatry at the Johns Hopkins University School of Medicine, conducted rigorous research on psychotherapy. In 1961, Frank published *Persuasion and Healing: A Comparative Study of Psychotherapy.* The book became a classic and went through two more editions (see Frank, 1973; Frank & Frank, 1991). The 1991 edition was coauthored by Julia Frank, Jerome's daughter. Jerome Frank died in 2005. In 2012, Julia Frank and Renato Alarcon published *The Psychotherapy of Hope: The Legacy of Persuasion and Healing*, a tribute to Jerome Frank's work. During his long tenure at Johns Hopkins, Frank focused his research on the question of what accounts for psychotherapy's effectiveness. His findings consistently showed that common factors found in all psychotherapies were the agents of effectiveness. The only exception to this general conclusion was that Frank thought certain desensitization techniques could, within themselves, be helpful to clients experiencing anxiety. According to Frank (Frank & Frank, 1991), the four features common to all psychotherapies are (a) an emotionally charged, confiding relationship with a helping person; (b) a healing setting; (c) a rationale, conceptual scheme, or myth that provides a plausible explanation for the client's symptoms and prescribes a ritual or procedure for resolving them; and (d) a ritual or procedure that requires the active participation of both patient and therapist and is believed by both to be the means of restoring the patient's health (pp. 38–44). On the basis of his research findings, Frank concluded that modalities and techniques, or what he called *rationales* and *rituals*, were important only as common factors. In other words, having a rationale and rituals is important but the specific rationale and rituals used are not that important. Thus, Frank was one of the first to demonstrate scientifically that common factors, not modalities and techniques, were the primary agents of change in psychotherapy.

Michael Lambert

Michael Lambert is a professor of psychology at Brigham Young University and a clinical psychologist in private practice. Lambert, who has served as president of the Utah Psychology Association, is editor of the fifth and sixth editions of the well-known *Bergin and Garfield's Handbook of Psychotherapy and Behavior* (Lambert, 2004, 2013). Lambert was one of the first researchers to show that client, therapist, and relationship factors are more potent determinants of outcome than techniques (e.g., Lambert, 1986; Lambert & Bergin, 1994). In 1986, Lambert published his well-known pie chart of the factors that account for therapeutic outcome. The chart, which was divided into four sections, showed that common factors account for 30% of outcome; techniques account for 15%; expectancy (placebo) accounts for 15%; and extratherapeutic change accounts for 40%. In other words, according to Lambert's chart, common factors are twice as potent as techniques. However, if one includes the client-related factors of expectancy (15%) and extratherapeutic change (40%) as common factors, then the total percentage is 85% (it's reasonable to include these as common factors because expectancy and extratherapeutic change are common to all psychotherapies). Thus, even using Lambert's chart, which was not based on meta-analysis but, rather, on an analysis of 100 studies that averaged effects of the factors in his chart, common factors (85%) are 5 to 6 times more potent than techniques (15%) in regard to outcome. Later, Wampold (2001a) published information based on meta-analysis of studies that indicated that specific treatments had even less effect than Lambert's chart had suggested. Wampold's analysis showed that specific modalities and techniques account for only 8% of the treatment variance and 1% of the total variance. Thus, according to both Lambert and Wampold, the specific treatment used makes relatively little difference. What really matters are common factors. They are by far the most potent agents of change in psychotherapy. Lambert, who has emphasized the importance of common factors for more than 30 years, is one of the modern "pioneers" of the common factors perspective. His contributions have changed our understanding of how and why psychotherapy works. Lambert continues to make major contributions to the common factors perspective. In recent years, he has focused attention on client feedback as a way to lower client dropout and increase effectiveness (e.g., Lambert, 2010a, 2010b; Lambert & Shimokawa, 2011). Both Lambert and Duncan (see a description of Duncan's contributions in this section) believe client feedback can have a significant impact on effectiveness and that routine gathering of such feedback should be a "common factor" in all therapeutic work.

Arthur Bohart

Arthur Bohart, a professor emeritus of psychology at California State University, Dominguez Hills, is perhaps best known for his emphasis on clients' active and creative processing of what they receive in therapy as the most potent determinant of therapeutic outcome (e.g., Bohart & Tallman, 1996, 1999, 2010). Although it has been generally acknowledged that the personal characteristics, degree of therapeutic participation, and extra-therapeutic aspects of clients' lives determine, more than any other factors, whether therapy will be successful, Bohart and Tallman went beyond this to argue that the real therapist in therapy is the client. The role of the therapist is to support and help mobilize the client's own intrinsic self-righting capabilities. This perspective, which places the client at the center of emotional healing, radically undermines the medical model with its emphasis on the knowledge and authority of psychotherapists and its assumption that modalities and techniques are the determinants of effectiveness. (For information on the potency of client factors, see the section on the human elements of psychotherapy in this chapter.)

Barry Duncan

In the early 1990s, Barry Duncan became involved with common factors as a full-time practitioner who was looking for ways to increase effectiveness and help as many clients as possible. Disenchanted by the "battle of the brands" and inspired by Lambert's (1986) common factors model, Duncan and colleagues (e.g., Duncan & Moynihan, 1994; Duncan, Solovey, & Rusk, 1992) believed that the best way to increase effectiveness was to apply what was known about psychotherapy outcome. Duncan proposed that clinicians spend time in therapy commensurate to each element's differential impact on outcome. Because the outcome research showed that client factors and the therapeutic alliance were powerful determinants of outcome, Duncan called on therapists to spend less time on models and techniques, which had relatively little effect on outcome, and more time supporting the inherent strengths of clients and building a positive therapeutic relationship. More specifically, Duncan called for a "client directed" approach that focused on clients' strengths and resources, clients' ideas on how they can be helped, clients' hopes and expectations about the therapy, and clients' views on the nature and quality of the therapeutic relationship. Duncan went on to publish 16 books and dozens of articles, as well as to conduct research on psychotherapy outcome. As an active clinician who has spent more than 17,000 hours in direct client contact, Duncan's major contribution, in my opinion, is his ongoing effort to operationalize the common factors in therapeutic work (see, e.g., Duncan, 2010b, 2014; Duncan, Hubble, & Miller, 1997; Duncan et al., 2004, 2010). Duncan believes that the client and the alliance are the "heart and soul" of change, a term he chose to name both the popular book about common factors (Duncan et al., 2010; Hubble et al., 1999) as well as the organization he directs (see https://heartandsoulofchange.com). Duncan's focus on the importance of privileging the client culminated in Partners for Change Outcome Management System (PCOMS), a client feedback system (see Anker, Duncan, & Sparks, 2009; Duncan, 2014). PCOMS solicits client feedback at each session about the outcome of therapy and the alliance to identify clients who are not responding to therapy. The feedback system helps clients, in collaboration with the psychotherapist, to find new and more helpful directions when the therapy is not going well. Duncan believes ongoing client feedback should be a common factor in all psychotherapies because of its proven effectiveness in helping clients to become more actively engaged in monitoring and improving their therapy experience, thus promoting more effective outcomes. (See Duncan, 2014, whose book *On Becoming a Better Therapist* shows how the activation of common factors in therapy, along with ongoing feedback from clients, can increase therapists' effectiveness.)

Mark Hubble, Barry Duncan, and Scott Miller

In 1999, Hubble, Duncan, and Miller edited *The Heart and Soul of Change*, a book that was destined to have a powerful impact on mainstream psychology's views as to why psychotherapy works. The book's basic message is that common factors, including the client, the therapist, and the alliance, are the major determinants of effectiveness in psychotherapy. The book was published by APA and reached a wide audience of clinicians, researchers, and students. In 2010, a second and updated edition was published with Bruce Wampold as a fourth editor (see Duncan et al., 2010). The second edition describes the latest thinking and scientific findings on the determinants of effectiveness. For example, there is a section describing therapist effects as well as a section on the importance of client feedback. The second edition continues to have an impact on clinical psychology's views on why psychotherapy works, as well as to provide guidance on how to be a more effective therapist.

Bruce Wampold

In the late 1990s, Bruce Wampold, who is now the Patricia L. Wolleat Professor of Counseling Psychology at the University of Wisconsin–Madison and director of the Research Institute at Modum Bad Psychiatric Center in Norway, entered the debate about psychotherapy effectiveness. When Wampold came on the scene, the debate was no longer about whether psychotherapy is effective. That had been settled since the late 1970s. Instead, the "great psychotherapy debate," as Wampold (2001a) called it in the title of his book, was about the factors that account for psychotherapy's effectiveness. As Wampold (2001a) pointed out, on one side of the debate are proponents of the medical model who believe that modalities and techniques account for psychotherapy's effectiveness. On the other side are those who believe that *contextual factors*, that is, common factors found in the context of all psychotherapies, account for psychotherapy's effectiveness. Wampold's research was designed to determine which side of the debate was right. To make this determination, he and his associates conducted analyses and meta-analyses of hundreds of published studies on psychotherapy effectiveness (see, e.g., Ahn & Wampold, 2001; Messer & Wampold, 2002; Waehler, Kalodner, Wampold, & Lichtenberg, 2000; Wampold, 2001a; Wampold et al., 1997). The findings were clear: Specific modalities and techniques had very little to do with effectiveness, whereas common factors were potent determinants of outcome. In 2001, Wampold published *The Great Psychotherapy Debate*, a book that gave a detailed summary of his research and findings. Near the end of the book, Wampold (2001a) stated his conclusion: "Clearly, the preponderance of the benefits of psychotherapy are due to factors incidental to the particular theoretical approach administered and dwarf the effects due to theoretically derived techniques" (p. 209).

Wampold's book helped ignite a revolution in clinical psychology. His findings showed that the medical model was wrong and that the common factors model was right. His findings also suggested that for more than a century clinical research, training, and practice had focused on the wrong factors in psychotherapy. If Wampold had published *The Great Psychotherapy Debate* in 2001 and then turned to other professional pursuits, the revolution might not have occurred. However, Wampold and his associates continued to do research on the determinants of effectiveness. Subsequent analyses and meta-analyses of additional studies confirmed the original conclusion: Common factors, not modalities and techniques, are the primary determinants of effectiveness in psychotherapy. For example, in 2008, Benish, Imel, and Wampold (2008) focused on posttraumatic stress disorder (PTSD). They conducted a meta-analysis on all studies published since 1989 comparing treatments of PTSD. The treatments included hypnotherapy, stress inoculation, exposure, cognitive, CBT, prolonged exposure, imaginal exposure, eye movement desensitization and reprocessing, and others. Despite longstanding claims that certain treatments for PTSD were more effective than others, the meta-analysis showed no differences in outcome between treatments. In other words, the specific modality and techniques of the therapist did not make a difference.

Then, in 2008, Miller, Wampold, and Varhely focused on children's disorders. They conducted a meta-analysis of all studies published between 1980 and 2006, comparing treatments for children with anxiety, depression, conduct disorder, and attention-deficit/hyperactivity disorder. Once again, the findings showed no differences in outcome between treatments.

Adding to this growing evidence, in 2008, Imel, Wampold, Miller, and Fleming conducted a meta-analysis of studies comparing treatments for alcohol abuse and dependence. The treatments included 12 Step, relapse prevention, CBT, and psychodynamic therapy. Once again, there were no differences in outcome between treatments.

It would be difficult to overstate the importance of Wampold's research. It is among the most impactful research on psychotherapy effectiveness that has ever been conducted. Wampold and his associates have now analyzed hundreds of published studies covering decades of psychotherapy research. The results are dramatically consistent: Specific modalities and techniques have little to do with effectiveness, whereas common factors are powerful determinants of change. Wampold's extensive and rigorous research places proponents of the medical model in a difficult position: Either they must acknowledge that psychotherapy's effectiveness is due primarily to common factors, not to modalities and techniques, or else they must conduct meta-analyses of their own to show that Wampold's conclusions were wrong. So far, such research has not been forthcoming.

William Stiles

William Stiles and his associates in the United Kingdom (see Stiles, Barkham, Mellor-Clark, & Connell, 2008; Stiles, Barkham, Twigg, Mellor-Clark, & Cooper, 2006) conducted a study of more than 5,000 psychotherapy clients. This was the largest study of psychotherapy effectiveness ever conducted in a "real-world" clinical setting. Clients received either cognitive–behavioral, person-centered, or psychodynamic treatment. The findings showed no differences in outcome between treatments. All three treatments were effective, and equally so. The 2006 study was criticized, so in 2008, another study was published that addressed the criticisms (Stiles et al., 2008). Once again, the results showed that all three psychotherapies were effective, and equally so.

THE HUMAN ELEMENTS OF PSYCHOTHERAPY

Among the common factors that contribute to effectiveness, the human elements are especially potent. This section presents examples of the human elements and their effect on outcome.

Client Factors

Client factors, which include what the client as a person brings to therapy, as well as the client's extratherapeutic experiences during therapy, account for 87% of the outcome variance, making client factors the most powerful determinant of therapeutic outcome (Bohart & Tallman, 1999, 2010; Duncan, 2010b; Duncan et al., 2004, 2010; Orlinsky et al., 2004). Fortunately, client factors are not static "givens." The personal strengths of the client can be supported and activated in therapy to increase effectiveness. Therapists can also influence the extratherapeutic experiences of clients. For example, they can encourage clients to engage in relationships and activities outside of therapy that promote improvement and personal growth.

Therapist Effects

Therapist effects are also potent, accounting for 5% to 8% of the variance of change and from 36% to 57% of the variance attributed to treatment (Duncan, 2014; see also Baldwin & Imel, 2013; Beutler et al., 2004; Crits-Christoph et al., 1991; Kim, Wampold, & Bolt, 2006; Wampold & Brown, 2005). Therapist effects are far more powerful than any treatment provided and are second only to client factors in potency (Duncan, 2010b). The therapist makes a difference. There are effective therapists and ineffective therapists. One of the differentiating variables between effective and ineffective therapists is empathy, one of the human elements of therapy. For example, when Lafferty, Beutler, and Crago (1989) examined effectiveness among trainees, they found that less effective trainees had significantly lower levels of empathy than more effective trainees. The researchers concluded, "The present study supports the significance of therapist empathy in effective psychotherapy. Clients of less effective therapists felt less understood by their therapists than did clients of more effective therapists" (Lafferty et al., 1989, p. 79).

Burns and Nolen-Hoeksema (1992) came to a similar conclusion. They examined therapist empathy in CBT therapists who were treating clients with depression. Describing their findings, the authors wrote, "The patients of therapists who were the warmest and the most empathic improved significantly more than the patients of the therapists with the lowest empathy ratings" (Burns & Nolen-Hoeksema, 1992, p. 447). As a result of this study, the CBT therapists at the clinic underwent empathy training and were required to ask clients to rate them on empathy at the end of each therapy session. Also, as noted earlier, Strupp and Hadley (1979) placed clients with either experienced psychotherapists or with professors who had no clinical training or experience but who were known for being warm and trustworthy. Clients in both groups improved, and equally so. These findings support the importance of the personal qualities and interpersonal abilities of therapists. Like client factors, therapist factors are not static. Therapists can become more effective by developing their personal qualities and interpersonal abilities. As Norcross (2010) wrote, "Therapists' relational contributions to outcome are identifiable and teachable" (p. 126).

The Therapeutic Alliance

The therapeutic alliance, meaning the interpersonal working relationship between the client and therapist, is also a potent factor in emotional healing (Horvath, Del Re, Flückiger, & Symonds, 2011). Orlinsky et al. (2004) noted that more than 1,000 studies have been conducted on the therapeutic alliance. According to Norcross (2010), "hundreds upon hundreds of research studies convincingly demonstrate that the therapeutic relationship makes substantial and consistent contributions to psychotherapy outcome" (p. 118). Hubble, Duncan, Miller, and Wampold (2010) said, "Researchers repeatedly have found that a positive alliance . . . is one of the best predictors of outcome" (p. 37). Summarizing findings on the alliance, Duncan (2010b) wrote,

> The amount of variance attributed to the alliance ranges from 5% to 7% of overall variance or 38% to 54% of the variance accounted for by treatment. Putting this into perspective, the amount of change attributable to the alliance is about five to seven times that of specific model or technique. (p. 23)

In a recent study of the therapeutic alliance as a causal factor in treatment outcome, Goldsmith, Lewis, Dunn, and Bentall (2015) found that the quality of the alliance, not particular techniques, determined outcome for 308 persons in an acute episode of early psychosis. The study showed not only that a good alliance was responsible for effectiveness but also that it's "actively detrimental" (p. 1) to continue treatment when the quality of the alliance is poor.

For years we have known that a good therapeutic relationship is important. More than 30 years ago, Yalom (1980) wrote that "the single most important lesson the psychotherapist must learn" is that "it is the relationship that heals" (p. 401). Yalom described the research that existed, even in 1980, on the importance of the therapeutic relationship:

> If any single fact has been established by psychotherapy research, it is that a positive relationship between patient and therapist is positively related to therapy outcome. Effective therapists respond to their patients in a genuine manner; they establish a relationship that a patient perceives as safe and accepting; they display a nonpossessive warmth and a high degree of accurate empathy and are able to "be with" or "grasp the meaning" of a patient. Several reviews that summarize hundreds of research studies concur in this conclusion. (p. 401)

In the last few decades, the evidence for the power of the therapeutic alliance has only increased. In 2002, the Task Force on Empirically Supported Therapy Relationships, a committee of Division 29 (Psychotherapy) of APA, documented the extensive evidence showing the importance of the therapeutic relationship. John Norcross, who chaired the task force, published an article in *Psychotherapy* (Norcross, 2001), as well as a landmark book (Norcross, 2002) summarizing that evidence. The work of the task force countered the emphasis on empirically supported treatments by showing the importance of what the task force called *empirically supported relationships.*

In contrast to the potent effects of the human elements of psychotherapy, the effects of differences among modalities and techniques are only about 1% of overall variance and 8% of the treatment variance (Wampold, 2001a). In other words, specific modalities and techniques have relatively little to do with effectiveness. As Duncan (2010b) wrote, "As long as the treatment makes sense to, is accepted by, and fosters active engagement of the client, the particular approach used is unimportant" (p. 24).

The bottom line is that the human elements of psychotherapy are the most powerful determinants of effectiveness. This undermines the medical model with its assumption that modalities and techniques are the instruments of change and calls for a new model of psychotherapy that places the human elements at the center of therapeutic work. As one of my doctoral students humorously put it, "Techniques are fine. The only problem is that they leave out the client, the therapist, and the relationship!"

CONCLUSION

The evidence presented in this chapter is foundation shaking to a profession that for more than a century has embraced the medical model with its assumption that modalities and techniques are the instruments of change. It's ironic that for decades clinical research, training, and practice marginalized the common factors, giving them "lip service" as nonspecific factors that have little to do with emotional healing. Now, the scientific tables have turned and the evidence shows that common factors are, in fact, the most potent determinants of effectiveness. To adapt a Biblical quotation, "The stone that the builders rejected has now become the cornerstone."

The evidence from clinical research, by itself, is sufficient reason to abandon the medical model and develop a nonmedical model of psychotherapy. However, the next two chapters, which present findings from other disciplines, provide even more evidence for a nonmedical model of emotional healing.

2

Attachment Theory and Social Relationships Research: The Power of Human Connection and Social Interaction

D rawing on findings from attachment theory and social relationships research, this chapter shows that we are evolutionarily hard-wired to develop, maintain, and restore our emotional well-being through supportive relationships with others. Thus, attachment theory and social relationships research enlarge our understanding of emotional healing and thus our understanding of how psychotherapy works.

ATTACHMENT THEORY

Attachment theory is an evidence-based theory that has been the focus of literally thousands of studies (Cassidy, 1999; Costello, 2013). Research on attachment theory is now being conducted in England, the United States, Canada, Italy, Germany, the Netherlands, and Japan (Brisch, 2011). This section defines attachment theory and describes its origins and development.

http://dx.doi.org/10.1037/14751-003
The Human Elements of Psychotherapy: A Nonmedical Model of Emotional Healing, by D. N. Elkins

Definition of Attachment

Referring specifically to the mother–child relationship, John Bowlby (1969), the founder of attachment theory, defined *attachment* as "an intense and enduring affectional bond that the infant develops with the mother figure" (p. 4). In a broader definition, Bowlby (1969) described *attachment* as "a lasting psychological connectedness between human beings" (p. 194). Mary Ainsworth (1969), who worked with Bowlby, gave the following definition: "Attachment refers to an affectional tie that one person (or animal) forms to another specific individual" (p. 971). Ainsworth (1969) also said that "attachment is a synonym for love" (p. 1008). Although definitions differ in focus or emphasis, the core meaning of the term is clear: Attachment refers to a close, caring, and enduring relationship.

Origins of Attachment Theory

Following World War II, the World Health Organization became concerned about orphaned and homeless infants and young children who, despite receiving basic physical care in institutional settings, were nevertheless developing serious physical and psychological problems. In 1949, the World Health Organization commissioned John Bowlby (1944, 1951, 1953, 1969, 1973, 1979, 1980, 1988), a psychiatrist who was head of the Department for Children and Parents at the Tavistock Clinic in London, to prepare a report on the problem. Bowlby reviewed the limited research that was available, consulted with developmental psychologists in Europe and America, and published his report in 1951. The report, titled *Maternal Care and Mental Health* (Bowlby, 1951), identified maternal deprivation as the problem. Bowlby described how staff in orphanages cared for the physical needs of infants and young children but otherwise left them socially isolated. He suggested that each infant and young child needed a consistent relationship with one primary caregiver: "The infant and young child should experience a warm, intimate, and continuous relationship with his mother (or permanent mother substitute) in which both find satisfaction and enjoyment" (Bowlby, 1951, p. 11). Having lost their biological mother, institutionalized infants and young children needed someone to take her place, a permanent mother substitute who would not only attend to the child's physical needs but also hold the child, comfort it, and socially interact with it. In short, Bowlby's report underscored the importance of human connection and social interaction for the healthy development of infants and children.

Although Bowlby's views seem like common sense today, many "child experts" of the time disagreed with his report. They found it hard to believe that caretaker–infant attachment could be as important as Bowlby suggested. During the first half of the 20th century, beliefs about child rearing were quite different from those held today. For example, during the Nazis' rise to power in Germany, Johanna Haarer (1934), a German physician, published *The German Mother and Her First Child*. The book, which instructed mothers on how to raise their child in line with National Socialist policy, was given to every new mother in Germany. The book emphasized the importance of letting infants experience frustration so as not to become spoiled. Mothers were told not to pick up a crying baby because frustration toughened the baby and crying strengthened the lungs. Following the Nazi era, the book, with its most blatant National Socialist ideology removed, remained popular in Germany. Indeed, the last edition was published in 1987 (Brisch, 2011). The idea that children should not be spoiled was a common view not only in Germany but also in other Western countries. Even today, parents are told not to spoil their child. Sadly, "Spare the rod and spoil the child" is an aphorism still used by some to guide child rearing practices.

While Nazis were telling German mothers to "toughen" their infants by letting them cry, child experts in the United States were also telling parents some strange things. For example, in a book on "scientific" child rearing, John Watson, the founder of behaviorism, advised parents as follows:

> Let your behavior always be objective and kindly firm. Never hug and kiss them, never let them sit in your lap. If you must, kiss them once on the forehead when they say good night. Shake hands with them in the morning. Give them a pat on the head if they have made an extraordinarily good job of a difficult task. (Watson & Watson, 1928, pp. 81–82)

In a chapter titled "Too Much Mother Love," Watson warned about the dangers of maternal affection. He told mothers,

> In conclusion won't you then remember when you are tempted to pet your child that mother love is a dangerous instrument? An instrument which may inflict a never-healing wound, a wound which may make infancy unhappy, adolescence a nightmare, an instrument which may wreck your adult son or daughter's vocational future and their chances for marital happiness. (Watson & Watson, 1928, p. 87)

Today, most parents would consider Watson's advice shocking or even abusive. Yet, even Benjamin Spock (1946; also see Maier, 2003), the famous "baby doctor" whose books were read by millions of parents during the 1940s and 1950s, advised parents not to pick up a crying baby but, instead, to let the baby "cry it out." (To his credit, Spock changed this advice in later editions of the book.) It also says something about society's view of children that during the Industrial Revolution, millions of children in both Europe and America, some as young as 7 years of age, worked 12-hour days in factories. Indeed, the first child labor laws were not successfully enacted in the United States until the late 1930s, following the Great Depression. In view of these cultural attitudes toward children and child rearing, it's not surprising that Bowlby's report was met with resistance.

Some of the strongest criticisms came from Bowlby's psychoanalytic colleagues (Bretherton, 1992; Mooney, 2010). Many psychoanalysts believed that mother–infant attachment derived from hunger and libidinal drives. In contrast, Bowlby said that the child's need for bonding with its mother was a primary motivation within itself. Bowlby's views also ran counter to those of Melanie Klein, who believed the internal "phantasies" of children were responsible for their responses (see Klein, 1932, 1975; Isaacs, 1948; Segal, 1980). Bowlby suggested that the focus should be on observations of how the child and parent actually interact. Bowlby's disagreements with mainstream psychodynamic theories eventually led to his being ostracized by his fellow psychoanalysts. Social learning theorists also disagreed with Bowlby. They believed the child's attachment to the mother was due to reinforcement and dependency. Bowlby acknowledged that reinforcement and dependency are involved in attachment, but he disagreed that they explained attachment. Instead, Bowlby posited internal "behavioral systems," sculpted by evolution, as being responsible for infant–mother attachment.

Despite the criticisms from various quarters, Bowlby's report had a significant impact on both professionals and laypersons. An abridged version of the report titled *Child Care and the Growth of Love* (Bowlby, 1953) was made available to the public. It was translated into more than a dozen languages and sold over 500,000 copies around the world. Today, Bowlby's report is considered a landmark in the history of psychology.

Development of Attachment Theory

Bowlby's hypothesis that infants and young children need a warm, intimate, and enduring relationship with one primary caregiver was the seed of what would become attachment theory. When Bowlby published his report in 1951, scientific research on child development was limited. Bowlby knew that if his hypothesis were to become a credible theory, he would need more evidence to support it. So in 1953 he hired Mary Ainsworth, a researcher who would help place attachment theory on a scientific foundation. Among other research projects, Ainsworth (1967) studied attachment between mothers and children in Uganda. She found that secure attachment in the Ugandan children was not determined by feeding or even by the mother's outward behaviors. Instead, secure attachment was an inward, emotional bond, an "affectional tie" between mother and child. Ainsworth was also responsible for the idea of a *secure base*, an important concept in attachment theory (see Bowlby, 1988). The term originated with William Blatz, a Canadian psychologist who had been one of Ainsworth's teachers (Wright, 1996). Ainsworth observed that children with secure attachments used their mother as a secure base, which allowed them to venture out and explore but to return to the mother for reassurance when needed. Ainsworth, Blehar, Waters, and Wall (1978) also developed the well-known Stranger Situation, which allowed researchers to classify attachment styles in children 12 to 18 months of age by observing how they reacted to the presence of a stranger. Four attachment styles were eventually identified: secure attachment, avoidant attachment, anxious attachment, and disorganized attachment. Ainsworth worked directly with Bowlby for more than 3 years and continued to collaborate with him for many years after that (Bretherton, 1992).

Bowlby's own efforts focused mainly on gathering evidence on mother–child attachment from numerous disciplines including ethology, evolutionary biology, cognitive science, developmental psychology, and psychoanalysis. Bowlby was especially impressed by the work of ethologist Konrad Lorenz (1970, 1971, 2007). Lorenz, who was awarded the Nobel Prize in Physiology or Medicine, had demonstrated that newly hatched geese have a brief window of time in which they attach to their mothers, or even to other moving objects in the immediate environment if the mother is removed. Lorenz called this *imprinting* and had famously demonstrated how baby geese whose mother had been removed imprinted on his boots and followed Lorenz whenever he wore the boots. Lorenz's studies showed that baby geese are evolutionarily primed to attach to their mother during this critical period after hatching. Bowlby viewed Lorenz's findings as relevant to his own work on mother–child attachment in humans. Although Bowlby did not believe that animal imprinting and human attachment were synonymous, he did believe that human infants, like Lorenz's baby geese, were evolutionarily primed to attach to a mother or mother substitute. From an evolutionary perspective, such attachment helped ensure the survival of the young. Thus, Lorenz's work provided an important link between attachment theory and evolutionary theory (see Ainsworth & Bowlby, 1991; Cassidy, 1999).

Bowlby's views received further support from Harry Harlow's (1958, 1962, 1964) research on rhesus monkeys at the University of Wisconsin. Harlow, who had been inspired to study maternal deprivation and attachment by Bowlby's 1951 report, found that baby monkeys separated from their mothers and kept in social isolation developed serious behavioral problems that could not be corrected when the monkeys became adults. When Harlow gave isolated baby monkeys a wire mesh or terry cloth "mother" to which they could cling, they fared better than isolated monkeys without such "mothers" but still exhibited serious deficits in social abilities. Interestingly, when Harlow allowed otherwise isolated young monkeys to interact socially for a few hours each day with another young monkey being raised normally, the isolated monkeys showed clear benefits from this limited social interaction. Harlow's extensive research on monkeys, one of our closest primate cousins, supported Bowlby's hypothesis that maternal attachment and social interaction are critical to the healthy development of infants and children. During the 1960s, Harlow, Bowlby, and Ainsworth had discussions about attachment and their respective investigations.

Bowlby and Ainsworth also had discussions with René Spitz. In the 1940s, Spitz (1945, 1946a, 1946b) had conducted systematic observations of infant development. As noted previously, most orphanages in those days attended to the basic physical needs of infants but otherwise left them isolated and alone in their cribs. Spitz showed that this lack of human connection and social interaction had devastating effects. In one of the first studies of infant development, Spitz (1946a, 1946b) compared a group of infants raised in an orphanage with a group of infants of prison inmates raised in prison. The infants in the orphanage were left isolated in their cribs. The infants in the prison interacted with their mothers on a daily basis as well as with prison staff. In addition, the cribs in the prison nursery were arranged so that the children could see one another. At 4 months of age, infants in the two groups showed no discernible differences. At the age of 1 year, however, children in the prison nursery showed clear signs of superior intellectual and motor development compared with the children in the orphanage. When the children were between 2 and 3 years of age, all of the children raised in the prison were able to walk, talk, and engage in age-appropriate social interactions. In fact, there were no developmental differences between the children raised in the prison and children who were raised in a normal family setting. In stark contrast, 24 of the 26 children raised in the orphanage were unable to walk or talk, and even the two who could walk could speak only a few words. None of the 26 children raised in the orphanage was able to interact socially in an age-appropriate manner. Spitz's study showed in dramatic fashion that human connection and social interaction are critically important to the healthy development of infants and young children.

For nearly two decades, Bowlby and Ainsworth conducted research, gathered evidence from various disciplines, and consulted with colleagues. Finally, in 1969, 18 years after his original report, Bowlby published *Attachment and Loss*. The book provided the first complete statement of attachment theory along with evidence supporting the theory. *Attachment and Loss* eventually grew into three volumes, with the final volume being published in 1980 (see Bowlby, 1969, 1973, 1980).

Extension of Attachment Theory to Adult Relationships

Originally, attachment theory focused on infants and caregivers, but later the theory was expanded to include adult relationships (see Ainsworth, 1991). The first studies of adult attachment focused mainly on romantic relationships (see, e.g., Hazan & Shaver, 1987, 1990, 1994; Simpson, 1990), but within a few years the focus expanded to include other adult relationships (see, e.g., Bartholomew & Horowitz, 1991; Grossman, Grossman, & Waters, 2005; Hart, 2010; Karen, 1998; Rholes & Simpson, 2004; Pietromonaco & Barrett, 1997; Trinke & Bartholomew, 1997). Today, attachment theory is a comprehensive, evidence-based theory that illumines all close relationships. The bond that Bowlby first observed in the mother–infant dyad has now become a prototype for all relationships in which intimate connection and social interaction are paramount. As Bowlby (1988) put it, "Attachment theory regards the propensity to make intimate emotional bonds to particular individuals as a basic component of human nature, already present in germinal form in the neonate and continuing through adult life into old age" (pp. 120–121).

Changes and Refinements to Attachment Theory

Over the years attachment theory has undergone changes and refinements. For example, in its early days attachment theory emphasized mother–child attachment and had little to say about fathers. This was later corrected by research showing that fathers are also important attachment figures and that in cultures in which child rearing is assigned to males instead of females, no differences in nurturing capacities were found (Field, 1978; Schaffer, 1996). Also, in a review and update of attachment theory, Rutter (1972, 1981) suggested that infant development is affected by many variables and that maternal deprivation should be considered a vulnerability factor instead of a causative agent. Finally, Kagan (2000) emphasized that attachment problems in infancy and early childhood are not deterministic. In other words, Kagan believed children could recover from early deprivations.

Despite the modifications to attachment theory, Bowlby's basic hypothesis has stood the test of time. Today, almost all developmental psychologists and other child-care specialists would agree that human connection and social interaction are critical to the healthy development of infants and young children and that the absence of these factors can have debilitating effects on children's physical, mental, emotional, and social development.

Attachment-Based Psychotherapies

In recent years, a number of attachment-based psychotherapies have been developed (see, e.g., Cassidy & Shaver, 2010; Costello, 2013; Sable, 2001; Wallin, 2007). Most of the therapies focus on identifying a client's "attachment style" and then tailoring the therapy to alter that style in a more positive direction. I believe these efforts are important as long as therapists don't become so focused on the "technical" task of identifying attachment styles and tailoring therapy to alter them that they forget what really heals in psychotherapy. Attachment theory shows that a deprived child needs a caretaker who is warm, caring, and empathic. The same is true for clients. So whatever approach we use in therapy, including attachment-based approaches, it's important that we provide clients with a warm, caring, and empathic relationship. Such a relationship is at the heart of all effective therapy.

The relevance of attachment theory to psychotherapy will be discussed in more detail following the next section on social relationships research.

SOCIAL RELATIONSHIPS RESEARCH

By the 1970s, scientists in various disciplines were conducting research on social relationships and health. If attachment theory showed that we develop emotional well-being through relationships, this research, which focused mainly on adults, showed that we maintain and restore emotional well-being through relationships. Some of the findings were striking, showing that we had seriously underestimated the power of human connection and social interaction.

Social Relationships and Physical Health

Perhaps the most dramatic finding was the association between social relationships and mortality (Berkman & Syme, 1979; Cohen, 2004; House, Landis, & Umberson, 1999). One of the first major studies on this topic was the Alameda County study. In 1965, residents of Alameda County, California, were invited to participate in a longitudinal study. The 6,928 participants completed questionnaires on their health, social ties, and other personal characteristics. They were followed at intervals for the next 20 years. In 1979, Berkman and Syme (1979) published a 9-year follow-up study that analyzed data on social networks and mortality. They found that the risk of mortality for males with the fewest social ties was 2.3 times greater than the risk for males with the most social ties. For females, the risk of mortality for those with the fewest social ties was 2.8 times greater than the risk for females with the most social ties. These findings were independent of participants' socioeconomic status, reported health status in the original survey, personal health practices, and use of health services. Commenting on the study, Cohen (2001) placed these findings in perspective: "The health risks of being isolated are comparable in magnitude to the risks associated with cigarette smoking, blood pressure, and obesity" (p. 2). The Berkman and Syme study sparked scores of additional studies on social relationships and mortality. Holt-Lunstad, Smith, and Layton (2010) conducted a meta-analysis of 148 of those studies, representing a total of 308,849 participants. The meta-analysis showed that those with stronger social relationships had a 50% greater likelihood of physical survival. This was true regardless of participants' age, sex, initial health condition, cause of death, or length of the follow-up period in the studies.

Not only do social relationships reduce the risk of mortality, they also act as a buffer against various medical conditions. Reviews of the research (see, e.g., Ertel, Glymour, & Berkman, 2009; Everson-Rose & Lewis, 2005; Uchino, 2006) show that higher quality and quantity of social relationships reduce the risk for high blood pressure, atherosclerosis, cardiovascular disease, myocardial infarction, cancer, and other medical conditions (Cohen, Doyle, Skoner, Rabin, & Gwaltney, 1997). By the beginning of this century, the evidence had become overwhelming that social relationships have a significant effect on physical and mental health. Reflecting this evidence, a report of the World Health Organization, edited by Wilkinson and Marmot (2003), stated the following:

> Social support and good social relations make an important contribution to health. Social support helps give people the emotional and practical resources they need. Belonging to a social network of communication and mutual obligation makes people feel cared for, loved, esteemed and valued. This has a powerful protective effect on health. (p. 22)

Today, there is general agreement in the scientific community that social relationships have a significant effect on health. Reflecting that consensus, Umberson and Montez (2010) wrote, "Solid scientific evidence shows that social relationships affect a range of health outcomes, including mental health, physical health, health habits, and mortality risk" (p. 61).

Social Relationships and Mental Health

As the statement by Umberson and Montez indicates, social relationships affect not only physical health but mental health as well. For example, Teo, Choi, and Valenstein (2013) conducted a 10-year follow-up study of 4,642 participants in the Midlife in the United States study. The study was one of the largest ever conducted on social relationships and depression. The results showed that the risk of depression for those with the lowest quality social relationships was more than double the risk for those with the highest quality relationships. Specifically, the researchers found that one in seven of those with the lowest quality relationships experienced depression during the 10-year follow-up period, whereas only one in 15 of those with the highest quality relationships became depressed. In another major study of relationships and depression, Mechakra-Tahiri, Zunzunegui, Preville, and Dube (2009) found that social support and healthy intimate relationships were associated with lower rates of depression among older adults in both urban and rural areas of Quebec.

Not only do social relationships help prevent emotional problems, but they also provide emotional healing when psychological problems do occur. For example, Schön, Denhov, and Topor (2009) studied 58 individuals who had recovered from severe psychological problems. They found that social processes and relationships were major factors in their recovery. The authors wrote, "The results show that recovery processes are social processes in which social relationships play a key role" (p. 347). Also, in a review of the international literature on social factors and recovery, Tew et al. (2012) concluded that social factors are at the heart of recovery from emotional difficulties.

The bottom line is this: The evidence from social relationships research, along with the evidence from attachment theory, shows that we are evolutionarily primed to develop, maintain, and restore our emotional well-being through relationships with others. This provides a new understanding of emotional healing and calls for a new model of psychotherapy that reflects the importance of human connection and social interaction.

RELEVANCE TO PSYCHOTHERAPY

The findings from attachment theory and social relationships research are highly relevant to psychotherapy. This section discusses some of the issues these findings illumine.

Why the Human Elements Are so Potent

Clinical research (see Chapter 1) has shown that the human elements are potent determinants of effectiveness but has not explained why this is so. Attachment theory and social relationships research fill this gap by showing that we are evolved to develop, maintain, and restore our emotional well-being through supportive relationships with others. Thus, the human elements of psychotherapy are effective because we are evolutionarily hard-wired to restore one another's emotional well-being through human connection and social interaction. From the perspective of attachment theory and social relationships research, it's really no surprise that the human elements of psychotherapy are the most potent determinants of effectiveness.

Although we know that the human elements are potent, we don't really know how they heal. In other words, we don't understand the complex processes that are involved. Clearly, this is an area where much research is needed. The following comments are speculative, but I hope they might generate ideas for investigation. First, the human elements may heal, in part, simply because they help provide a sense of safety and security for a client who is in distress. Humans evolved in a social context where the presence of trusted others provided safety and helped ensure survival. Thus, psychotherapy may offer a relational sanctuary that, within itself, contributes to the client's emotional healing.

Second, the human elements may heal by activating the attachment system. Bowlby (1988) said that when a person engages in caregiving behaviors on behalf of another, this can activate the attachment system. More recently, Fonagy, Bateman, and Luyten (2012) wrote, "A sensitive therapist responding humanely to interpersonal distress and exploring its causes will trigger the psychological system selected over millennia to generate a powerful affectional bond" (p. 34). Thus, the same relational power that operates in infancy and childhood to help develop emotional well-being may also operate in psychotherapy to help restore emotional well-being.

Third, the field of mentalizing (see Allen & Fonagy, 2006; Allen, Fonagy, & Bateman, 2008; Bateman & Fonagy, 2012) may provide clues as to how the human elements heal. Mentalizing, which is both a clinical theory and a therapeutic focus, has roots in attachment theory and relational psychodynamic theory. Bateman and Fonagy (2012) defined *mentalizing* as "our ability to attend to mental states in ourselves and in others as we attempt to understand our own actions and those of others on the basis of intentional mental states" (p. xv). According to the theory, the ability to mentalize develops in childhood in the context of secure attachments. However, if a child has insecure attachments, this ability can be compromised, causing emotional and social difficulties. As Bateman and Fonagy asserted, "Without mentalizing, there can be no robust sense of self, no constructive social interaction, no mutuality in relationships, and no sense of personal security" (p. xv). For clients who did not develop the ability to mentalize in childhood, psychotherapy can reactivate the attachment system and provide them with another opportunity to develop the ability in the context of the therapeutic relationship (Bateman & Fonagy, 2012). In other words, like attachment between a mother and child, attachment between a therapist and client can provide the relational milieu that is needed to develop the ability to mentalize. As clients grow in this ability, they can better understand and regulate their own internal states and interact with others in more effective and satisfying ways. Thus, according to proponents, mentalizing is essential to emotional and social well-being, and the human and relational elements of psychotherapy provide the milieu in which the ability can develop.

Fourth, an intersubjective perspective may help explain how the human elements heal. In 1987, Stolorow, along with coauthors Brandchaft and Atwood, published *Psychoanalytic Treatment: An Intersubjective Approach.* The book had a major impact on psychodynamic theory and treatment, as well as on other therapeutic approaches. Intersubjectivity is based in a post-Cartesian, Heideggerian philosophical perspective that rejects the subject–object split of the Cartesian view. Cartesian thinking leads us to view the client and therapist as two separate, enclosed "subjectivities" who influence each other in linear fashion through back and forth exchanges, somewhat like two tennis players hitting a tennis ball back and forth. Stolorow believed this is Cartesian thinking that limits our understanding of what is actually taking place in psychotherapy. Taking a post-Cartesian perspective, he believed the client and therapist are immersed in an intersubjective field that is constituted by a blending of their two experiential worlds. Because the therapist cannot stand outside this field as an objective observer, the focus of psychotherapy, of necessity, is on the phenomena of the relational field. As Atwood and Stolorow (1984) put it, "Clinical phenomena cannot be understood apart from the intersubjective contexts in which they take form. Patient and analyst together form an indissoluble psychological system, and it is the system that constitutes the empirical domain of psychoanalytic inquiry" (p. 64).

Cartesian thinking tends to reify relational processes, turning them into "things" that can be observed and studied. For example, empathy is a complex relational process that is sometimes reified as though it were a healing thing among other healing things such as caring, respect, acceptance, and so on. Yet, the truth is, it is extremely difficult—probably impossible—to isolate empathy from other relational processes because they all blend together into a dynamic, fluid, and ever-changing field in psychotherapy. Consequently, a therapist's "empathic response" to a client tends to be a blend of empathy, caring, respect, acceptance, and perhaps other healing elements. It would be a researcher's nightmare to try to isolate each healing element from the others and determine its particular contribution to the client's emotional healing. According to Wampold (2010), "the common factors mutually influence each other over time and thus form a complex system that is difficult to understand, let alone research" (p. 96). Thus, instead of reifying dynamic processes and trying to isolate specific healing elements, I suspect it would be more productive to adopt a post-Cartesian perspective that focuses on the nature and quality of the intersubjective field. The dictum of the gestalt psychologists that "the whole is more than the sum of its parts" seems particularly true in regard to the intersubjective field of psychotherapy.

Ainsworth's (1967) observations of attachment in Uganda point to the usefulness of an intersubjective perspective. When Ainsworth studied attachment in mothers and children in Uganda, she observed that secure attachments did not seem to be the result of specific behaviors by the mothers. Instead, secure attachments were characterized by an emotional bond between mother and child. Ainsworth coined the term *affectional tie* to describe that bond. The presence or absence of that emotional bond, not specific behaviors on the part of the mother, determined whether the attachment was secure or insecure. I suspect that the emotional bond that Ainsworth observed was the intersubjective field created by a blending

47

of the experiential worlds of each mother and child. Thus, there was no "standardized formula" of maternal behaviors that could produce secure attachments because each mother and child was unique and the blending of their subjectivities was a creative process.

The same is true for psychotherapy. There is no standardized formula of therapist behaviors that can reliably produce a healing attachment between client and therapist. Instead, each therapist and client creatively blend their experiential worlds to produce a unique intersubjective field. Thus, psychotherapy is an art that can never be reduced to a standardized formula. Each client and therapist dyad creates a unique intersubjective field, and the nature and quality of that field, not choreographed therapist behaviors, will determine whether the client's emotional well-being is nourished and restored. So if we want to understand how the human elements heal, I suspect we will need to focus more research on the nature and quality of the relational field.

Why a Variety of Psychotherapies Are Effective

The findings presented in this chapter also explain why a variety of psychotherapies are effective, and equally so (see Chapter 1). Proponents of the medical model, who believe modalities and techniques are the instruments of change, have difficulty explaining why various psychotherapies, which differ widely in modalities and techniques, are effective. The only reasonable explanation is that common factors found in these therapies are the primary agents of change. Thus, any psychotherapy where these factors are present in a robust way is likely to be effective. However, if medical-model proponents acknowledge this, then they must also acknowledge that the medical model is scientifically flawed and that for more than a century clinical research, training, and practice have focused on the wrong factors in psychotherapy. In the past, clinical psychology marginalized the human elements of psychotherapy. This is no longer a viable scientific position. It is time to acknowledge what the evidence shows: Common factors, and particularly human factors, are the major determinants of effectiveness in psychotherapy, and specific modalities and techniques have relatively little to do with effectiveness. Thus, modalities and techniques are the factors that should be marginalized. Indeed, they are so inherently impotent that it doesn't really matter which modality and techniques a therapist uses, as long as they match the client's needs and inspire therapeutic engagement. Thus, what we once thought was marginal is central, and what we thought was central is marginal.

A New Understanding of Psychotherapy

Perhaps the most important contribution of attachment theory and social relationships research is a new understanding of emotional healing and thus a new understanding of psychotherapy. From the perspective of these disciplines, psychotherapy can be conceptualized as a special type of human connection and social interaction that restores the client's emotional well-being. We need to demystify psychotherapy and stop obfuscating its real nature by describing it in medical and technical terms. Psychotherapy, properly understood, is simply a relationship between a client who is in emotional pain and a therapist who is able and willing to help. This is not to equate psychotherapy with common, everyday relationships but, rather, to emphasize that psychotherapy is cut from the same cloth. Psychotherapy is effective because it draws on the power of human connection and social interaction to restore the client's emotional well-being.

To make this discussion more concrete, consider a typical therapy experience. For an hour or more each week, a client goes to psychotherapy where she experiences empathy, support, and care. There she can talk openly about the intimate fabric of her life; about her relationships and emotional pain; and about her triumphs, hopes, and dreams. She knows that she will not be judged, that she will be accepted and understood. In this powerful milieu of human connection and social interaction, she finds healing for her emotional pain and new possibilities for her life.

We must never underestimate the power of this kind of experience. When we are in emotional pain, nothing is more healing than talking with someone who is empathic, caring, and supportive. We are social creatures and we need one another, and even more so when we are hurting or going through a difficult time. Thus, psychotherapy is a special relationship in which clients experience the healing power of human connection and social interaction with a therapist who knows how to support and activate this healing power to restore the client's emotional well-being.

Qualities of an Effective Therapist

The findings from attachment theory and social relationships research also illumine the qualities of an effective therapist. Because humans are evolved with the ability to give and receive emotional healing through social means, most emotional healing does not occur in a psychotherapist's office. Instead, it occurs through connections and interactions with family members and friends. In that sense, we are all healers and, at times, in need of healing. When our child pours out her heart about a stressful problem at school and we listen with empathy and concern, it's likely that a degree of emotional healing will take place. When we ourselves are demoralized, many of us find comfort in talking to our spouse, partner, or friend. Millions of such "small healings" take place every day throughout the world. At times, however, talking to a family member or friend is not enough. Because of the nature or severity of the problem, or perhaps for some other reason, the distraught person decides to seek professional help. It is estimated that 10 million Americans receive psychotherapy every year (Wang et al., 2005, 2006). Therapy is provided by a wide range of professionals, including psychologists, marriage and family therapists, licensed clinical social workers, psychiatrists, and others. The information presented in this chapter suggests that a professional therapist, at least an effective one, is a person who is talented in the art of healing through social means. In every society and historical period there are individuals who have special talent in certain fields. For example, there are the "Michelangelos" in art, the "Beethovens" in music, even the "Michael Jordans" in sports. The same is true in regard to the art of healing through social means. Some individuals, through innate abilities, life experience, formal training, or a combination of these, are especially talented in the art of healing through social means. Ideally, psychotherapists should be selected from this elite group. This is not to suggest that all psychotherapists must be Michelangelos, Beethovens, or Michael Jordans, but that they should be individuals who have special talent in the art of healing others through human connection and social interaction. Thus, psychotherapists are not "junior physicians" wielding medical-like techniques. Instead, they are warm, empathic, caring healers who know how to connect and interact with clients to heal their pain and restore their emotional well-being. Obviously, this view of the role and function of psychotherapists has important implications for the selection and training of therapists, a topic that is discussed in Chapter 5.

CONCLUSION

Findings from attachment theory and social relationships research show that we are evolved to develop, maintain, and restore our emotional well-being through human connection and social interaction and that psychotherapy is an expression of this evolutionarily derived ability. We are evolutionarily hard-wired to heal and be healed by human connection and social interaction. Thus, the human elements are the "power center" for emotional healing in psychotherapy. Without those elements, psychotherapy could not heal. Prior to attachment theory and social relationships research, we did not know the power of human connection and social interaction. Now that we know, we need a model of emotional healing that reflects this knowledge. Thus, attachment theory and social relationship research lay another foundation stone for a nonmedical model of psychotherapy.

3

Neuroscience and Evolutionary Theory: How Our Brains Are Evolved to Heal Through Social Means

Most of us who practice psychotherapy are not accustomed to thinking about what we do in neurobiological terms. We know, of course, that psychiatric medications affect the client's brain, but we think of psychotherapy as the "talking cure," a psychological approach that is radically different from administering brain-altering drugs. The truth, however, is that psychotherapy also alters the client's brain. In fact, as Benedetti (2011) and others (e.g., Cozolino, 2014, 2010; Grawe, 2007; Kandel, 1998; Kandel, Schwartz, & Jessell, 2000) have reminded us, no changes can occur in the client's behavior, thoughts, or emotions without changes in the client's brain. Numerous studies, using special imaging techniques, have documented significant neural changes during or following psychotherapy (e.g., Fu et al., 2008; Goldapple et al., 2004; Ipser, Singh, & Stein, 2013; Kumari et al., 2011; Martin, Martin, Rai, Richardson, & Royall, 2001;

http://dx.doi.org/10.1037/14751-004
The Human Elements of Psychotherapy: A Nonmedical Model of Emotional Healing, by D. N. Elkins

Prasko et al., 2004; Schienle, Schäfer, Stark, & Vaitl, 2009; Straube, Glauer, Dilger, Mentzel, & Miltner, 2006).

Thus, from a neurobiological perspective, the talking cure is actually a brain-altering process. However, instead of using psychiatric medications to change the client's brain, psychotherapy uses what Wampold (2012) called *social means* (p. 445). The term *social means* refers to the social factors in psychotherapy, or what this book calls the *human elements*. These are the social means that change the client's brain and bring about emotional healing.

Neuroscience is important to psychotherapists because, among other reasons, it helps us to understand how the talking cure heals. Ironically, neuroscience, a biological discipline often associated with the medical model, actually supports a nonmedical model of psychotherapy by showing that our brains are evolved to give and receive emotional healing through social means.

THE WONDERS OF NEUROSCIENCE:
A CAUTIONARY COMMENT

Before going further, I want to mention some cautions about the use of neuroscience and its findings. First, it is important for us as clinicians and clinical scientists not to oversimplify complex findings from neuroscience and use them inappropriately to support a pet theory or ideology. Satel and Lilienfeld (2013) rightly warned against "the oversimplification, interpretive license, and premature application of brain science in the legal, commercial, clinical, and philosophical domains" (p. 6). Neuroscience is still in its infancy and new discoveries, some of which will be relevant to psychotherapy, will be made as the future unfolds. Nevertheless, at this point we already have reliable, if limited, information about the neurobiology of the doctor–patient relationship and how emotional healing takes place. I will be conservative in describing these findings and their clinical implications in this chapter.

Second, another danger associated with neuroscience is reductionism. Reductionism does not necessarily arise from oversimplification or misapplication of neuroscientific findings but, rather, from an inflated admiration of the field. Neuroscience is popular, and some of its findings about the human brain are indeed remarkable, even awe inspiring. As a result, it is easy to become so enamored with neuroscience that we are tempted to think that neurobiological descriptions are the only legitimate descriptive systems for human experience. For example, it's tempting to describe such human phenomena as love, hope, and altruism in terms of brain structures, circuitry, and chemistry. Although such descriptions are indeed fascinating and perhaps even accurate from a neurobiological perspective, it is easy to forget that there are other descriptive systems, equally valid, that place these important human experiences in a phenomenological context, describing them in terms of the meaning and value they hold for human beings. Indeed, perhaps the greatest danger with the current fascination with neuroscience may be the tendency to describe important human experiences in material, biological terms without also acknowledging their subjective, value-laden, and phenomenological dimensions. This is not to deny that all human experiences have neurological substrates but, rather, to affirm that in our scientific age, biologically based explanations can push aside other ways of knowing that are just as valid and sometimes more important to human life. For example, it would be unthinkably reductionistic to describe a mother's love for her child in terms of neural activity and brain chemicals without also recognizing that her subjective and value-laden experience of love for her child, a phenomenological experience, is a vital component of any full and accurate description of parental love. Therefore, as we review the findings of modern neuroscience, many of which are indeed remarkable, I hope our enthusiasm for biological explanations will be tempered by the realization that, as human beings, we live in more worlds than one.

A BRIEF HISTORY OF THE HUMAN BRAIN AND ITS STUDY

The human brain is one of the most complex organs ever produced by evolution. The neuron is the basic unit of the nervous system, and according to recent research, the adult human brain contains about 86 billion neurons (Azevedo et al., 2009; Herculano-Houzel, 2009). Through billions of axons and tentacle-like extensions called dendrites, neurons form elaborate net-works with other neurons, connecting the various parts of the brain and shaping and reshaping neural networks throughout life. Of course, basic structures of the brain, along with much of their neural circuitry, are already in place at birth, but during our long developmental period from infancy to adulthood, the human brain adds billions of neurons and countless neural networks to make increasingly complex thoughts, emotions, and behaviors possible.

Most ancient cultures considered the brain unimportant. For example, the ancient Egyptians thought the heart, not the brain, was the seat of intelligence. They considered the brain merely a "stuffing" for the cranium (Brüne, Ribbert, & Schiefenhövel, 2003). In an early Egyptian papyrus, dated ca. 17th century BCE, an unknown Egyptian physician likened the brain to "slag" (Finger, 1994, p. 7; see also Breasted, 1991; Finger, 2000; Nunn, 1996; Sullivan, 1996). The Greek physician Hippocrates (ca. 460–370 BCE) is usually credited with being the first to suggest that the brain, not the heart, was responsible for mental abilities. However, Aristotle (384–322 BC), who lived during the same "Golden Age" of Greece (ca. 500–300 BCE), continued to insist that the heart was the seat of intelligence and that the brain was simply a cooling system for the body (Finger, 1994). During the Roman period, Galen (129–216 AD), a physician who treated wounded gladiators, noted that those who sustained brain damage often suffered the loss of certain mental abilities. Galen also conducted studies on the brains of animals and concluded, in agreement with Hippocrates, that the brain, not the heart, was the seat of mental abilities (Nunn, 1996).

During the European Renaissance, science slowly replaced Church dogma as the dominant epistemology in the West, and it became increasingly acceptable to study the human body, including the brains of cadavers. Andreas Vesalius, a Renaissance physician who is often called the founder of modern anatomy, did extensive dissections of human cadavers and carefully mapped some of the basic structures of the brain. Also, in the late 1500s, the optical microscope, an instrument that would eventually become critical to studying the brain, was invented. Two Dutch spectacle makers, Hans Zaccharias and his son Janssen, are often given credit for its invention (Bradbury, 1967; Finger, 1994). However, it was nearly a century later, in the second half of the 1600s, before extensive studies of biological tissue using the microscope were conducted. Even then, brain tissue was so dense that it was impossible to distinguish the minuscule structures that we now know as neurons, axons, and dendrites. Finally, in the second half of the 19th century, nearly 300 years after the invention of the microscope, Camillo Golgi, an Italian physician and scientist, discovered a tissue-staining method that allowed the minute structures of brain tissue to be seen under the microscope (Mazzarello, Badiani, & Buchtel, 2010). Santiago Ramon y Cajal, a Spanish neuroscientist, using a microscope and Golgi's staining method, which he improved on, was able to identify neurons as the fundamental unit of nerve tissue (see Cajal, 1996; Finger, 2000). In 1906, Golgi and Cajal were jointly awarded the Nobel Prize in Physiology or Medicine for their discovery and categorization of neurons.

During that same period, Paul Broca (1824–1880), a French physician and surgeon, focused his research on brain-injured patients who exhibited symptoms of aphasia. His patients were either partially or totally unable to speak, write, read, name familiar objects, or understand the meaning of spoken language. Broca discovered that these disabilities were due to lesions in the left frontal cortex of the brain. Broca's research provided the first anatomical proof of localization of brain function, which was a major scientific breakthrough.

During the early years of the 20th century, scientists were able, for the first time, to produce detailed models of the brain that showed various brain structures and the functions they controlled. In the mid-20th century, Bernard Katz (1966, 1969), a German neurophysiologist, studied neurotransmission and synapses, opening up a line of research that continues today. In 1970, Katz was awarded the Nobel Prize in Physiology or Medicine for his contributions.

The real heyday of neuroscience, however, has been the last 25 years. As the 20th century entered its final decade, the National Institute of Mental Health and the Library of Congress dubbed the 1990s the Decade of the Brain. That decade saw a dramatic increase in neuroscientific research and discoveries. One of the most important discoveries was that the human brain is always a "work in progress." We are not born with all the brain cells and neural circuitry that we will eventually have. Instead, our brains are incomplete at birth and continue their development outside the womb. From infancy to late adolescence, the brain adds billions of new cells and neural circuits that are shaped by experience, especially social experience. Even in adulthood and old age, the brain continues to change, adding new cells and circuits that are shaped by experience.

This *neural plasticity*, as neuroscientists call the brain's ability to change, has important implications. It means that throughout our lives, the brain continues to change. Even more remarkable, it means that the brain, a biological organ, can be influenced and shaped by social experience. As Cozolino (2010) wrote, "The human brain is a 'social organ of adaptation' stimulated to grow through positive and negative interactions with others. The quality and nature of our relationships become encoded within the neural infrastructure of our brains" (pp. 12–13). This helps us to understand how psychotherapy works. From a neuroscientific perspective, psychotherapy can be conceptualized as a special type of social experience that changes the client's brain. Old neural circuits are modified, and new circuits are created. This is not accomplished by drugs, surgery, electroshock, or other such medical procedures. Instead, it is accomplished by the talking cure. Psychotherapy is possible because our brains are evolved with the ability to give and receive emotional healing through social means. This is why the human and relational elements of psychotherapy are so potent and also why modalities and techniques have relatively little effect. We are evolved with the ability to heal one another's brains through social means. Thus, what really matters in therapy are the social factors, what this book calls the human elements of psychotherapy.

Neuroscience has come a long way from the time of the ancient Egyptians who thought the brain was stuffing for the cranium to the contemporary view that the brain is the site of all mental abilities. From a historical perspective, the neuroscience "train" moved slowly for centuries, if it moved at all. Then in the 19th and 20th centuries, the train began to pick up speed. Finally, in the past 25 years, the train has become almost a bullet train, traveling at record speeds for a scientific field. Today, there are thousands of neuroscientists around the world and several hundred universities, research centers, and institutes that are dedicated to brain research. The Society for Neuroscience, the largest neuroscience association in the world, has more than 40,000 members representing more than 80 countries. Other organizations include the Federation of European Neuroscience Societies, the International Brain Research Organization, and such national associations as the British Neuroscience Association, the German Neuroscience Society, and the French Society of the Neurosciences. Because of the field's dramatic growth, along with advances in related fields such as molecular biology and brain imaging, neuroscience will continue to make important discoveries about the brain, many of which will be relevant to clinical psychology.

EVOLUTION OF THE "SOCIAL BRAIN"

About 6 million years ago, our primate ancestors began to evolve separately from the other apes. Over hundreds of thousands of years, their brains slowly evolved, becoming larger and having mental abilities that no other animals had. But why did our species evolve to have larger brains and complex mental abilities? One of the most plausible answers to this question is the social brain hypothesis (SBH).

The Social Brain Hypothesis

Jolly (1966) and Byrne and Whiten (1988) were the first to suggest that the larger brains of primates, including humans, might be due to the demands of social complexity. Later, Dunbar (see Dunbar, 1988, 1998, 2009; Shultz & Dunbar, 2012) formalized this idea into the SBH. Dunbar and Shultz (2007) defined the SBH as follows:

> The essence of the SBH is that the need to solve (ecological) problems in a social context, rather than in a demographic vacuum, imposes significant cognitive demands. Within a social environment, individual decisions must be responsive to the decisions made by other group members and the constraints these impose. (p. 649)

The SBH is based on the view that evolutionary processes operate in response to the demands of the social environment as well as to those of

the physical environment. Thus, as the social environment of our ancestors became more complex, their brains became larger and developed
mental abilities to deal with that complexity. In turn, larger, more socially
capable brains were able to create even more social complexity, which
demanded even more neurological development. Thus, this "evolutionary
dialogue" between increasing social complexity and increasing neurological development eventually produced the human brain with its complex
mental abilities. That, in essence, is what the SBH proposes.

The SBH has gained acceptance not only because a great deal of evidence supports it but also because it's congruent with evolutionary theory.
Natural selection and other evolutionary processes operate in the interest
of survival. Group life, with its social complexity, would have given our
ancestors an edge in that regard. To survive, our nomadic ancestors had to
find and gather roots, berries, nuts, and other forms of plant life; they had
to stalk and kill wild animals for meat; they had to locate streams, lakes,
springs, and other sources of water; and they had to protect themselves
from predators. To accomplish these tasks, all of which were essential for
survival, group life offered advantages. Forty brains and bodies are better
than one when it comes to locating and gathering food, stalking and killing wild animals, locating sources of water, and fighting off predators. At
the same time, group life also made demands. Group members had to learn
how to think, plan, organize, communicate, collaborate, and be willing to
place the welfare of the group above their own immediate self-interests.
Thus, from an evolutionary perspective, it makes sense that increasing
social complexity over millions of years would have produced larger brains
with more complex mental abilities. As Viamontes and Beitman (2012)
said, "Living in social groups has been a highly adaptive strategy for the
human species, and millions of years of natural selection have refined the
tools necessary for success in the social realm" (p. 52).

The Social Brain and Psychotherapy

The term *social brain* is increasingly being used to describe those structures, functions, and characteristics of the human brain that are associated with social behavior (see, e.g., Brüne, Ribbert, & Schiefenhövel, 2003;

Costa & O'Leary, 2013; Cozolino, 2010; Dunbar, Gamble, & Gowlett, 2010; Graziano, 2013; Hood, 2012; Legerstee, Haley, & Bornstein, 2013). The term reflects the view that the human brain developed in a social context in which physical survival depended on the evolutionary sculpting of a brain that could engage in increasingly complex social behavior. Because of this evolutionary history, we now have a social brain, meaning a brain that has the ability to engage in sophisticated social behavior.

What does this have to do with psychotherapy? The fact that we have a social brain makes psychotherapy possible. The social brain equips therapist and client to engage in the complex social interactions of psychotherapy. The social brain makes empathy, trust, collaboration, compassion, acceptance, and other such social factors possible. And because the social brain evolved with the ability to change in response to social experience, the client's brain can change in response to the intense and focused "social experience" of psychotherapy, thus making emotional healing possible. As Cozolino (2010) said,

> Because we know that relationships are capable of building and rebuilding neural structures, psychotherapy can now be understood as a neurobiological intervention, with a deep cultural history. In psychotherapy we are tapping the same principles and processes available in every relationship to connect to and heal another brain. (p. 305)

THE EVOLUTION OF HEALING

Healing is an important part of evolutionary history. I use the word *healing* to refer to the self-healing capabilities of the human body and brain and also to the healing that occurs through the presence and actions of others on behalf of the sick or injured.

Evolution of Self-Healing

In the interest of survival, evolution provided us with biological mechanisms and processes designed to prevent illness and injury as well as mechanisms and processes designed to promote healing when we do become ill or injured. For example, the most primitive parts of the brain "prevent" us from dying by regulating heartbeat, blood pressure, breathing, body temperature, and other vital functions under varying conditions. Our immune system prevents illness by warding off life-threatening microorganisms. The fight–flight response helps us to survive when we confront external dangers. In short, our brains and bodies are evolutionarily hardwired to promote survival by preventing illness and injury.

Despite these preventive mechanisms and processes, however, we do become ill and injured at times. Fortunately, evolution has also provided us with mechanisms and processes that promote self-healing. For example, if we become ill because of a bacterial or viral disease, our immune system attacks the invading microorganisms to help us heal. Even when we break a bone, tear a ligament, or sustain a serious wound, healing mechanisms and processes are immediately activated. Although a physician may set the bone, repair the ligament, or stitch the wound, no healing would occur without the self-healing capabilities of the patient's body and brain.

Self-healing has evolved throughout the natural world in both animals and plants. For example, when lobsters lose a claw, they grow a new one. When sharks break off a row of teeth, they quickly grow a new set. Even a tree, damaged by lightning or a woodcutter's ax, heals its "wound" by covering it with new bark. Self-healing is ubiquitous; it is one of evolution's most widely distributed gifts.

Evolution of Healing by Others

It is likely that healing by others evolved in response to the demands of group life as did other socially oriented capabilities. A severely ill man cannot go on the hunt. A woman with a broken leg cannot gather nuts and berries. Thus, the ability to heal one another was important for both individual and group survival. So at some point in evolutionary history our ancestors began to offer assistance to the ill and injured. Instead of watching them die or leaving them behind, they tried to help. Perhaps they brought food and water to them. Maybe they helped them walk, or even carried them, on their nomadic journeys. The earliest physical evidence of social assistance is the toothless skull of a hominin who lived 1.7 million years ago and survived for at least 2 years after becoming toothless. Anthropologists believe he may have been fed by others who mashed his food so he could eat it (see Lordkipanidze et al., 2005). Although we don't know exactly when or how healing by others began, we do know *that* it began and that it evolved over time to become a major part of group life. As healing became ubiquitous among our ancestors, their brains changed in response to this important part of group life. Thus, the evolution of the social brain, which gave us other socially oriented capabilities, also gave us capabilities related to healing one another.

The Shaman as Healer

Eventually, the shaman, or tribal healer, arose as an important figure in group life. Perhaps our ancestors found it more efficient or effective to designate one person to be responsible for healing. As is true in many traditional cultures today, shamans were probably selected on the basis of the group's perception that they had special abilities related to healing. Also, because our ancestors were animistic, shamans were likely selected because they were believed to have special powers to influence the spiritual world on behalf of ill or injured persons (Eliade, 1964). As far as we know, our ancestors did not differentiate among physical, psychological, and spiritual illness. Thus, the shaman was healer of body, mind, and spirit. Only later did these shamanistic functions differentiate into physician (healer of the body); psychotherapist (healer of the mind); and pastor, rabbi, or other religious leader (healer of the soul or spirit). Although the shamanistic tradition is an important part of our past, the tradition arose quite late in evolutionary history. For hundreds of thousands of years, healing among our ancestors was done by "laypersons," that is, by members of the group who took an interest in the sick or injured person. Even after the rise of shamanism, members of the group were still responsible for the daily care of the injured or ill. Thus, all of our ancestors, not just shamans, were involved with healing. This is why the human brain, over evolutionary expanses of time, developed capabilities related to giving and receiving healing.

HEALING THROUGH SOCIAL MEANS

Healing through social means represents an evolutionary addition to the healing capabilities discussed previously. Because the concept is central to understanding how psychotherapy heals, I discuss it in some detail.

Definition of Healing Through Social Means

The term *healing through social means* refers to our evolutionarily derived ability to heal one another through certain types of social behaviors, connections, and interactions. Healing through social means is a relatively new concept, so it's important to expand on that definition to clarify what the term means and doesn't mean. For example, healing through social means does not mean that healing is done *in* a social context but, rather, that healing is done *by* the social context. In regard to psychotherapy, the social factors of therapy, what this book calls the human elements, are themselves the instruments of healing. Physicians heal through surgery, drugs, and other "medical means" but psychotherapists heal through social means, that is, through certain types of social behaviors, connections, and interactions. One could say that psychotherapy is a special type of social experience that is specifically designed to heal emotional pain. Because the human brain evolved with the ability to change in response to social experience, the intense social experience of psychotherapy alters clients' brains, thus healing their emotional pain and restoring their emotional well-being. To put it another way, psychotherapy draws on our evolutionarily derived power to heal one another emotionally through social means and uses that power to heal the client. This is what it means to heal through social means.

How Healing Through Social Means Evolved

It's likely that our ability to give and receive emotional healing through social means has evolutionary roots in our more general need to give and receive healing to help ensure survival, as discussed previously. As our ancestors gave and received healing over hundreds of thousands of years, the brain developed complex neural networks specifically related to heal-ing. Remarkably, some of those networks evolved in such a way that they could be activated simply by healing-oriented social behaviors and inter-actions. This is the evolutionary origin of the placebo response. Although healing by social means is a broader concept than the placebo response, it's nevertheless important to understand this unusual phenomenon. It's really quite remarkable that the mere sensory and social stimuli of a heal-ing situation, absent the administration of any effective treatment, can activate self-healing mechanisms and processes in the patient's brain and body. In medicine, the placebo response often has negative connotations because, historically, many bogus treatments were based on the placebo response. Also, in medical research, scientists must overcome the placebo response to demonstrate the effectiveness of a new drug or medical tech-nique. Thus, in medicine, the placebo response is viewed as an obstacle to be overcome. However, when one considers the placebo response from a neurobiological perspective, it's another fascinating capacity of the human brain and body. That's why neuroscientists (e.g., Benedetti, 2008, 2011; Benedetti & Amanzio, 1997) are studying the neurobiological mechanisms and processes involved in this healing-related phenomenon. As neuroscientists learn more about the placebo response and how it's activated, this information could help psychotherapists in their efforts to support and activate self-healing capabilities in clients.

Although the placebo response is active in psychotherapy, it would be a mistake to conclude that healing through social means is nothing but the placebo response. Healing through social means *includes* the pla-cebo response but goes far beyond it. Healing through social means draws on the broader neurobiological mechanisms and processes involved in human connection and social interaction. For example, as documented in Chapter 2, attachment theory shows that human connection and social interaction between a child and caregiver have potent effects on the physi-cal and emotional development of the child. Clearly, this is not the placebo response. Instead, it's the expression of complex neurobiological processes that evolved in the interest of survival. Further, as also documented in Chapter 2, social relationships research has shown that the quantity and quality of our relationships help maintain and restore our physical and emotional well-being. Indeed, relationships are so potent that they can have an effect on whether we live or die. Again, this is not the placebo response. The point is this: There is something about social relationships that has a powerful effect on our emotional well-being and this "something" is not simply the placebo response. Once this is understood, we can begin to focus clinical research on the human and relational aspects of psychotherapy to increase our understanding of exactly how this potent something restores the client's emotional well-being.

Psychotherapists and Healing Through Social Means

Although we don't normally use the term *social means*, those of us who practice psychotherapy heal through social means all the time. In fact, we know a great deal about how to do this. For example, we know (a) how to structure a healing therapeutic situation; (b) how to develop a good client–therapist relationship; (c) how to tailor our approach to the client's personal and cultural needs; (d) how to extend empathy, support, and care in ways that are healing; and (e) how to seek and use client feedback to make therapy more effective. In fact, therapists are so skilled at healing through social means that 80% of those experiencing emotional difficulties who go to therapy are better off than those who don't (Duncan, 2014; Wampold, 2001a). Psychotherapy's robust effectiveness has been attained despite the fact that clinical research has focused primarily on modalities and techniques, which have relatively little to do with effectiveness. If more research were focused on the factors that are primarily responsible for emotional healing, it's likely that psychotherapy would become even more effective.

OTHER FINDINGS RELEVANT TO PSYCHOTHERAPY

In recent years, numerous scholars have discussed the contributions of neuroscience to psychotherapy (e.g., Arden, 2015; Badenoch, 2008; Benedetti, 2011; Cozolino, 2010, 2014; Etkin, Phil, Pittenger, Polan, &

Kandel, 2005; Ivey & Zalaquett, 2011; Schore, 2012; Siegel, 2007, 2012; Tryon, 2014; Viamontes & Beitman, 2012). This section describes some of those contributions.

Meeting the Doctor

Perhaps most of us have had the experience of going to the doctor when we were not feeling well and noticing that we felt better even before any treatments were administered. There is a neurobiological reason for this. Because our brains are evolved to give and receive emotional healing through social means, even the act of meeting the healer can activate neural pathways associated with healing (Benedetti, 2011).

In regard to psychotherapy, this finding suggests that emotional healing can begin at the first contact between therapist and client. For psychotherapists, meeting new clients can become a routine part of clinical practice, but "meeting the doctor" is often a significant and emotionally charged event for a new client. From a neuroscience perspective, the first meeting is important because it can activate healing processes in the client's brain.

The Ritual of the Therapeutic Act

Like meeting the doctor, the ritual of the therapeutic act can have a significant effect on the client's brain by activating neural pathways associated with hope and expectancy. In fact, in studies of psychiatric medications, it's sometimes difficult for researchers to determine whether the drug or the ritual of the therapeutic act is responsible for improvement. For example, Benedetti et al. (2003) conducted a study of patients with anxiety. When the patients were given diazepam without knowing the drug had been administered, they experienced no anxiety-relieving effects. Then a doctor administered an inert substance in an open manner and assured patients that it would relieve their anxiety. Remarkably, it did so.

This is where modalities and techniques come in. Although modalities and techniques have little *inherent* power to heal, they are nevertheless important as part of the ritual of the therapeutic act. Jerome Frank (Frank & Frank, 1991) emphasized that modalities and techniques, which he called rationales and rituals, are common features of all psychotherapies, and in that role, they contribute to emotional healing. From the perspective of neuroscience, modalities and techniques are part of the ritual of the therapeutic act and thus have an effect on the client's brain. As Benedetti (2011) put it, "The therapeutic act activates expectation and placebo mechanisms that are at the very heart of the therapeutic outcome" (p. 49).

Mirror Neurons

Mirror neurons were discovered in 1992 by a group of neuroscientists (see di Pellegrino, Fadiga, Fogassi, Gallese, & Rizzolatti, 1992). Mirror neurons are a special type of neurons that fire in the brain of an observer as he or she watches another individual perform an action (Iacoboni, 2009; Keysers, 2011). The pattern of firing in the observer's brain is similar to the pattern in the brain of the actor. Thus, the observer's neurons "mirror" the neurons of the individual who is actually performing the action. In addition, the firing of mirror neurons activates areas of the observer's brain that are associated with affective processing (see Carr, Iacoboni, Dubeau, Mazziotta, & Lenzi, 2003; Phan, Wager, Taylor, & Liberzon, 2002). Thus, the observer's neurons not only mirror neurons related to the action, they also activate emotions associated with the action.

The discovery of mirror neurons is important to psychotherapy because they appear to be associated with the evolutionary development of empathy and "mind reading" (Domes, Heinrichs, Michel, Berger, & Herpertz, 2007). *Mind reading* refers to our ability to imagine what another person is thinking and feeling. In psychotherapy, mirror neurons in the therapist's brain mirror the neural patterns in the client's brain and activate related emotions in the therapist. These patterns and processes in the therapist's brain provide an internal reference point that helps the therapist to understand what the client is experiencing. Like the vibrations of a tuning fork that set off the same vibrations in another tuning fork, the neural patterns in the client's brain cause the therapist's brain to "vibrate" in a similar pattern. Thus, it's likely that mirror neurons are at the heart of our ability as therapists to imagine what our clients are experiencing. This, of course, is the essence of empathy, which we know is an important factor in emotional healing. Mirror neurons help us to understand the neurobiological substrates of this important therapeutic factor.

Oxytocin

Oxytocin is a neuropeptide that was discovered in 1906 by Sir Henry Hallett Dale, a British pharmacologist, who found that oxytocin promoted uterine contractions in women giving birth. A few years later, Ott and Scott (1910) and Schafer and MacKenzie (1911) found that oxytocin also promoted mother–child bonding and helped mothers to "let down" their milk to nursing babies. In recent years, neuroscientists have focused on oxytocin's effect on relational variables and prosocial behavior. Although the research is ongoing and results are sometimes mixed, it appears that oxytocin promotes prosociality as well as empathy and trust (see Beckes & Simpson, 2012; Decety & Ickes, 2011; Domes, Heinrichs, Michel, Berger, & Herpertz, 2007; Gordon, 2009; Kosfeld, Heinrichs, Zak, Fischbacher, & Fehr, 2005; Neumann, 2008). Summarizing the research on oxytocin, Beckes and Simpson (2012) said that the results show "clear evidence for the powerful role of oxytocin in care giving behavior" (p. 41). Interestingly, bonding, prosociality, and caregiving in humans appear to be based in neural mechanisms and processes associated with parent–child attachment, including the release of oxytocin (see, e.g., Goetz, Keltner, & Simon-Thomas, 2010; Richerson & Boyd, 1998, 2005). In other words, the same neural processes that promote mother–child bonding also promote adult-to-adult bonding. Thus, from an evolutionary perspective, it appears that the original purpose of oxytocin was to promote mother–child bonding in the interest of survival but that its purpose was extended to promote adult-to-adult relationships, also in the interest of survival. The research on oxytocin converges with findings from attachment theory and social relationships research that our brains are evolved to promote human connection and social interaction throughout the life span. Other mammals also produce oxytocin. Nagasawa, Kikusui, Onaka, and Ohta (2009) conducted an experiment in which they asked dog owners to engage in petting sessions with their dogs. Oxytocin levels increased in dogs and their owners following the sessions. This suggests that oxytocin plays a role in the bonding that occurs between dogs and their owners. It may also help explain the positive effects of therapy dogs on patients who are ill or infirm.

What is the role of oxytocin in psychotherapy? Because oxytocin is associated with empathy, trust, and care giving behavior, it may play a role in the development and maintenance of the therapeutic relationship. Of course, the client–therapist relationship is a complex and deeply human experience. It cannot be, and should not be, explained as nothing more than the effects of a neuropeptide. Such an explanation would be reductionistic and far too limited. Nevertheless, the research on oxytocin may provide a neurobiological perspective on the development of the therapeutic relationship, which is a potent factor in emotional healing.

Empathy and Compassion

Benedetti (2011) suggested that empathy may have evolutionary roots in mutual grooming behavior among our ancestors. To groom another requires a focus on the needs and preferences of the other. The experience of self-grooming, which likely occurred earlier in evolutionary history, may have provided an internal sense of what feels good and is effective. Thus, groomers may have used their own internal reference point to help them imagine what the other needed. In time, this empathic sense of the needs of another, which developed in mutual grooming, may have generalized into imagining what others are thinking and feeling in other situations. The ability to imagine what another is thinking and feeling is, of course, at the heart of empathy (Iacoboni, 2009).

Although compassion and empathy are probably related, neuroimaging shows that compassion follows different neural pathways (Goetz,

Keltner, & Simon-Thomas, 2010). If empathy involves imagining how another person is thinking and feeling, compassion seems to go a step further. It has an active, prosocial element that may be its distinctive feature. In compassion, but not necessarily in empathy, one is inspired to act in an effort to relieve another's difficulty or pain.

Anxiety and Depression

Anxiety and depression are common psychological problems. Although we have much to learn about the neurological substrates of these problems, we know that psychotherapy is highly effective in healing anxiety and depression. In fact, psychotherapy is often as effective as drugs, without the risk of side effects, and psychotherapy clients are more resistant to relapse (Hollon, Stewart, & Strunk, 2006; Imel, Malterer, McKay, & Wampold, 2008; Wampold, 2010). Unfortunately, most clinical research has focused on techniques designed to alleviate anxiety and depression, and little research has focused on how the social factors of therapy affect clients with these problems. I suspect that if clinical scientists focused on the social factors, they would find that these factors have a great deal to do with psychotherapy's effectiveness in healing anxiety and depression.

Emotional Pain

Eisenberger and associates at University of California, Los Angeles, have conducted studies on the neurological correlates of the emotional pain associated with social rejection (see, e.g., Eisenberger & Lieberman, 2004). Brain imaging suggests that the emotional pain of social rejection follows some of the same neural pathways associated with physical pain. This led Eisenberger to conjecture that in our evolutionary development, attachment may have co-opted the neural pathways of physical pain to help ensure survival. A "broken heart" that is due to social rejection can be just as painful as a broken bone. As therapists, we should keep this in mind.

CONCLUSION

This chapter has shown that the human brain evolved in a social context with remarkable abilities, including the ability to change in response to social experience and the ability to heal other brains through social means. From a neurobiological perspective, psychotherapy can be conceptualized as a special type of social experience that changes the client's brain and restores the client's emotional well-being. Thus, the chapter has laid another "foundation stone" for a nonmedical model of psychotherapy by showing that it is the social factors, not specific modalities and techniques, that make the real difference in psychotherapy.

4

Moral Treatment:
A Historical Example of Healing
Through Social Means

In the 1800s, a new treatment arose in Europe and spread to America. The treatment was reported to be highly effective and launched an era of optimism that those with severe psychological problems could be cured. Thousands of patients sought treatment, filling existing hospitals and asylums as new ones were being built. The name of the approach was *moral treatment*. Unlike the medical treatments of the day, moral treatment was humane and used social means to help those with psychological problems.

This chapter discusses moral treatment as a historical example of healing through social means. The chapter is divided into three sections. First, I describe treatments before moral treatment; second, moral treatment itself; and third, the end of moral treatment and the rise of biological treatments in the 1900s.

http://dx.doi.org/10.1037/14751-005
The Human Elements of Psychotherapy: A Nonmedical Model of Emotional Healing, by D. N. Elkins
Copyright © 2016 by the American Psychological Association. All rights reserved.

TREATMENTS BEFORE MORAL TREATMENT

To provide historical context for the rise and spread of moral treatment in the early 1800s, this section describes religious treatments during the Middle Ages and medical treatments during the 1700s.

Religious Treatments

During the Middle Ages of Europe (ca. 500–1500), the Catholic Church was considered the source of truth, and mental disturbance was typically viewed through the lens of the Church's teachings. If "treatments" were offered, they tended to be religious in nature, ranging from prayer, to exorcism, to burning "witches" at the stake. Those with severe mental disturbance were often viewed as demon possessed, and the treatment of choice was exorcism.

During the Inquisition, women who exhibited symptoms of hysteria, epilepsy, or schizophrenia were often accused of being witches (Chodoff, 1982; Porter, 1998; Veith, 1965). In 1486, two Dominican priests, Heinrich Kramer and James Sprenger, published the *Malleus Maleficarum*. The term has been translated into English as *"the hammer of witches"* (see Mackay, 2009; Summers, 1971). The book presented guidelines on how to identify and prosecute witches. For the next 2 centuries, *The Hammer of Witches* was used to put thousands of "witches" to death. Witches were viewed as agents of the Devil who could cast spells on individuals and even entire communities, so they were considered especially evil and dangerous. Normal legal procedures were sometimes suspended so that inquisitors could exact a confession by torturing women accused of witchcraft. No one knows how many women were killed, but scholarly estimates range from 45,000 to 60,000 (Roper, 1994). Levack (2006), a scholar on the European witch hunts, estimated that there were about 90,000 prosecutions and 45,000 executions. Hutton (1999), another scholar, placed the estimate at 60,000 deaths. Women convicted of being witches were not necessarily put to death; some were imprisoned or banished. In some jurisdictions, the execution rates were as low as 25%, whereas rates in other jurisdictions were as high as 90% (Levack, 2006). The misogyny in *The Hammer of*

Witches is extreme. Although the authors acknowledge that men can also be involved in witchcraft, they make it clear that "there are more women than men infected with the heresy of witchcraft" (Summers, 1971, p. 47). For this, the authors praised God, saying, "And blessed be the Highest who has so far preserved the male sex from so great a crime" (p. 47). Although such misogyny, along with other factors, fueled the Church's long and bloody oppression of women, many of the victims were targeted because of their psychological problems.

Medical Treatments in the 1700s

As the Middle Ages came to an end and the Renaissance spread across Europe, Church teachings were slowly replaced by more secular perspectives. The responsibility for treating those with psychological problems passed from the Church to the medical community and from priests using religious rituals to physicians using medical treatments. In 1684, Thomas Willis, an English physician, published one of the first medical texts on "madness." The title was *The Practice of Physick: Two Discourses Concerning the Soul of Brutes* (R. Whitaker, 2002). The Age of Reason (ca. 1650–1790) was dawning in Europe, and the prevailing philosophy was that the ability to reason is what separates humans from animals. Because the mad had lost their ability to reason, Willis believed they had descended to the level of animals, or "brutes." Thus, they had to be controlled and "broken." Willis's views influenced other physicians so that during the 1700s, treatments for the insane focused on controlling the brutes and on inflicting pain and fear that, it was believed, could sometimes cause them to return to their senses. Such treatments were often combined with biological interventions deemed appropriate by the treating physician. Although physicians acknowledged that their treatments were harsh, they insisted that such methods were necessary to cure those who had descended into madness. Some of the treatments are described next (for more information on treatments, see Porter, 2004; Rush, 1812/1962; Scull, 1989; Shorter, 1997; and R. Whitaker, 2002).

Blood-Letting, Purges, Emetics, and Blistering

During the 1700s, physicians used blood-letting, purges, emetics, and blistering to treat the "mad." Benjamin Rush, often referred to as the first American psychiatrist, was especially fond of blood-letting (Brodsky, 2004). Rush (1812/1962) believed madness was caused by disordered actions of the blood vessels in the brain. He thought mania was caused by too much blood circulating in the brain so draining blood from the patient's body would reduce the amount flowing to the brain, thus calming the blood vessels there. Rush said that he had cured many patients using the procedure.

Purges and emetics produced extreme nausea, vomiting, and diarrhea and were often continued for weeks or even months (R. Whitaker, 2002). Rush (1812/1962) claimed that purges "often bring away black bile, and sometimes worms" and that "emetics, by exciting the stomach, often remove morbid excitement from the brain, thus restoring the mind to its healthy state" (p. 100).

Blistering often involved shaving the patient's head and then rubbing mustard powder into the scalp (Kendell, 2001). Once blisters formed, a caustic agent was then rubbed into the blisters and the raw skin underneath. The pain was excruciating, and the treatment often went on for months. Physicians said that blistering could cure madness, and so the treatment, even though painful, was ultimately for the patient's own good (Kraepelin, 1962).

Mechanical Contraptions: The Swinging Chair, Tranquilizing Chair, and Gyrator

During the 1700s, physicians invented various mechanical contraptions to treat the mad. The swinging chair involved strapping a patient into a chair and rotating it at a high speed, sometimes as much as 100 revolutions per minute. The spinning, which often went on for hours, caused anxiety, nausea, vomiting, urination, defecation, fatigue, and sometimes cerebral hemorrhage. Physicians claimed the treatment had a positive effect on the patient's thinking, breaking up old thought patterns and causing patients to have new thoughts (R. Whitaker, 2002).

Benjamin Rush, whose penchant for blood-letting was discussed previously, invented the tranquilizing chair. Patients were strapped into the chair so that their limbs were immobilized. The head was also confined by a box-like device that restricted the patient's vision. A bucket was attached underneath so patients could urinate and defecate through a hole in the bottom of the chair. Describing the benefits of the chair, Rush said, "In 24, 12, six and in some cases in four hours, the most refractory patients have been composed" (Scull, 1989, p. 69).

Rush also invented the gyrator, a bed-like machine on rollers that could be spun around the room. Rush believed melancholic patients had insufficient blood circulation in the brain. Thus, the gyrator was the ideal treatment. The patient was strapped to the "bed," which was then spun around the room at high speeds. The centrifugal force sent blood rushing to the patient's head, thus increasing circulation in the brain.

Hydrotherapy: The Bath of Surprise and "Drowning" the Patient

Hydrotherapy was a common treatment for madness. As the term suggests, it involved the use of water. One hydrotherapy treatment was the "bath of surprise." The patient, not knowing what was in store, was blindfolded and placed on a platform over a trap door. The door was then sprung, and the patient plummeted into a tank of cold water below. Physicians claimed the sudden shock often restored the patient's sanity.

The most terrifying hydrotherapy treatment involved locking a patient in an iron cage and then lowering the cage into a pond (see R. Whitaker, 2002). When the bubbles stopped and the patient was almost drowned, the cage was lifted out of the water and the patient was revived. Physicians said that if patients are "drowned" and then brought back to life, this could cause them to start a new life, leaving their madness behind (Jimenez, 1987).

As the previous discussion indicates, during the Middle Ages priests had no idea what caused emotional problems, and in the 1700s, physicians were just as clueless. Unfortunately, this did not deter them from developing strange theories and brutal treatments. This was the historical context in which moral treatment arose.

MORAL TREATMENT

Near the end of the 1700s, cultural attitudes toward the mad became more humane. The Age of Reason (ca. 1650–1790) was ending and the Romantic Period (ca. 1785–1832), with its emphasis on the "affections," was beginning. Reform was in the air, and changes were initiated at various asylums in Europe. For example, in Florence, Italy, Vincenzo Chiarugi, a physician, led reforms that included outlawing the use of chains to restrain the mad (Gerard, 1998; Mora, 1959). The most influential reformer of this period was Philippe Pinel (1745–1826). Pinel liberated patients from chains at two Paris hospitals and formulated the basic principles of a more humane approach to treating the insane. In the 1800s, the treatment would become famous in Europe and spread to America. The name of the approach was *moral treatment.*

Definition of Moral Treatment

Pinel (1801) used the French term *traitement moral* to describe his approach. The term was translated into English as *moral treatment.* The English term is confusing because the English word *moral* has strong ethical implications and does not accurately convey Pinel's meaning. The French word *moral,* while having ethical connotations, referred primarily to the passions, emotions, or affections. Adding to the confusion, moral treatment, as made famous by the Quakers at the York Retreat in England, placed heavy emphasis on ethics. Some scholars (e.g., Grange, 1961; Jones, 1996) have suggested that Pinel used the French word *moral* to refer to the emotions, whereas the Quakers used the English word *moral* to refer to ethics. However, as Charland (2007) pointed out, this is an oversimplification because moral treatment, in both Pinel's conception and in its Quaker manifestation, contained both affective and ethical components. It is true, however, that the Quakers at the York Retreat added their own brand of religious and ethical values to moral treatment. For example, the Quakers read the Bible to patients and invited them to attend religious services. In his *Description of the Retreat,* Samuel Tuke (1813/1996), the grandson of the retreat's founder, said that "the influence of religious principles over the mind of the insane, is considered of great consequence, as a means of cure" (p. 161). Also, as Charland (2007) pointed out, the rules of the retreat emphasized five Quaker values that are ethical in nature: benevolence, charity, discipline, self-restraint, and temperance.

When Pinel originally formulated *traitement moral*, he would never have imagined that the ethical component would include the religious and moral teachings of the Quaker religion. This is not to say that those teachings were of no benefit to the patients at the York Retreat but, rather, that Quaker teachings are not essential features of moral treatment. In fact, when moral treatment spread to secular settings, the Quaker teachings were not included and the treatment continued to be effective.

As the previous discussion suggests, moral treatment is not easy to define. Even the name is misleading, and the Quaker additions muddy the definitional waters even more. However, I believe the following definition, which is based on descriptions by Pinel (1806/1962) and Tuke (1813/1996), captures the essential features of the approach: Moral treatment is a therapeutic approach that has both affective and ethical components, both of which are requisite features of the treatment. In regard to the affective component, moral treatment focuses on the passions, emotions, or affections of patients. In regard to the ethical component, patients, to the best of their ability, are expected to work, engage in orderly and disciplined behavior, and participate in personal and cultural activities designed to enhance their well-being. Attendants are expected to treat patients with kindness and respect and never hit them. They are to view patients as equals. They are to eat with them, talk with them, listen to their concerns, and offer them social and emotional support. Moral treatment is not a psychotherapy, although it has implications for psychotherapy. Instead, it's a *milieu therapy* in the sense that patients are part of a supportive social environment and participate in activities designed to enhance their physical, mental, and emotional well-being.

Origins of Moral Treatment

Philippe Pinel is usually considered the founder of moral treatment because he was the first to formulate and publish its basic principles (see Pinel, 1799,

1806/1962). Pinel is typically remembered for liberating patients from their chains, but his contributions to treatment have received less attention. Therefore, it seems important to provide information about Pinel and his *traitement moral.*

As a youth, Pinel received a literary education and planned to pursue religious studies. However, after studying theology for a while, he decided to become a physician and enrolled in the Faculty of Medicine at the University of Toulouse. Pinel received his MD degree in 1773, and in 1778, he moved to Paris, where he would remain for the rest of his life. During the French Revolution (1789–1799), the new government appointed Pinel to care for patients at Bicêtre Hospital, the hospital for men in Paris. Bicêtre housed 4,000 men, including 200 on the insane ward. Before the revolution, the insane had been locked up in asylums, and many were chained to the floors or walls of their cells. The asylums were unheated, filthy, and a breeding ground for disease. Patients were fed starvation rations, and their beds were typically straw spread on the floor of their cells. At Bicêtre Hospital, more than half of those admitted to the insane ward died of hunger, cold, or disease within the first year.

When Pinel arrived at Bicêtre, he took special interest in the patients on the insane ward. He discovered that Jean-Baptiste Pussin, the director of the ward, had already begun to make reforms. Instead of using whips and prods, Pussin talked with patients and treated them with kindness and respect. The patients responded by being more orderly and trying to do what Pussin asked. Pinel was so impressed by Pussin's management style that he apprenticed himself to Pussin to learn from his approach (Weiner, 1979). As Pinel observed how patients improved in response to Pussin's kindness and respect, he realized that he was observing not only a more humane management style, but also a more effective approach to treatment. As Pinel (1806/1962) put it,

> I then discovered that insanity was curable in many instances by mildness of treatment and attention to the state of the mind exclusively, and when coercion was indispensable, that it might be very effectively applied without corporal indignity. (p. 108)

Pinel began to formulate what would become his *traitement moral.* He rejected the idea that patients were brutes that had to be controlled. Pinel believed patients could be reached through their emotions, their affective capacity. They may have lost their minds, but they had not lost their hearts. So instead of using treatments that induced pain and terror, Pinel treated patients as human beings. He talked with them, got to know them, and treated them with respect. In this caring environment, patients improved. In fact, some improved so much that they were able to be discharged. In a moving tribute that shows his respect for patients, Pinel (1806/1962) wrote,

> I have nowhere met, except in romances, with fonder husbands, more affectionate parents, more impassioned lovers, more pure and exalted patriots, than in the lunatic asylum, during their intervals of calmness and reason. A man of sensibility may go there every day of his life, and witness scenes of indescribable tenderness. (p. 16)

As part of his reforms, Pinel wanted to liberate patients from their chains. To do this, however, he had to convince city leaders that removing patients' chains would not endanger others. In one of his early experiments, Pinel invited a city leader to join him as an observer on the insane ward. For the experiment, Pinel chose a patient who had been in chains for 40 years. The patient, an English sea captain, was considered especially dangerous. Earlier, he had killed an attendant by striking him in the head with his manacle. Conolly (1847) described what happened:

> Pinel entered his cell unattended, and calmly said to him, "Captain, I will order your chains to be taken off, and give you liberty to walk in the court, if you will promise me to behave well and injure no one." "Yes, I promise you," said the maniac, "but you are laughing at me; you are all too much afraid of me." "I have six men," answered Pinel, "ready to enforce my commands, if necessary. Believe me on my word, I will give you your liberty if you will put on this waistcoat." He submitted to this willingly, without a word; his chains were removed, and the keepers retired, leaving the door of the cell open. He raised himself many times from the seat, but fell again on it, for

he had been in a sitting posture so long that he had lost the use of his legs; in a quarter of an hour he succeeded in maintaining his balance, and with tottering steps came to the door of his dark cell. His first look was at the sky, and he cried out enthusiastically, "How beautiful!" During the rest of the day he was constantly in motion, walking up and down the staircases, and uttering exclamations of delight. In the evening he returned of his own accord into his cell, where a better bed than he had been accustomed to had been prepared for him, and he slept tranquilly. During the two succeeding years which he spent in the Bicêtre, he had no return of his previous paroxysms, but even rendered himself useful, by exercising a kind of authority over the insane patients, whom he ruled in his own fashion. (p. 165)

Pinel left Bicêtre in 1795 to become head physician at Salpêtrière Hospital, the hospital for women in Paris. Salpêtrière housed 6,000 patients, 600 on the insane ward. Pinel offered Pussin a job at the new location and the two continued working together until Pussin's death in 1811. Pinel developed a following of young physicians and medical workers who, even after his death, continued to spread his ideas on moral treatment across Europe.

Traitement Moral

Pinel first used the term *traitement moral* in 1799 in an article titled *Recherches et observations sur le traitement moral des alienes* (Pinel, 1799). As the title indicates, the article described Pinel's research and observations on treating the insane. In 1809, he published *Traité medico-philosophique sur l'aliénation mentale ou la Manie*, which is now available in English under the title *Medico-Philosophical Treatise on Mental Alienation* (see Pinel, 1809/2008). The book describes the basic features of *traitement moral*. In the book, Pinel rejected many of the medical treatments of the day including blood-letting, hydrotherapy, and "the practice of striking deranged patients as a mean of curing them" (p. 3). Pinel emphasized the importance of giving patients individualized attention and always treating them with kindness and goodwill. He also underscored the importance of personal hygiene, daily exercise, and meaningful work for patients. These were the essential ingredients of his *traitement moral.*

Because Pinel worked in hospitals that housed hundreds of patients, he could not fully implement *traitement moral.* For example, it was impossible for him to provide the level of personal attention and meaningful activities that he believed patients needed. Nevertheless, Pinel implemented *traitement moral* to the degree possible, and the changes he saw in patients convinced him that the treatment was effective. However, the first full implementation of moral treatment, and thus the first real experiment to see if it worked, was at the York Retreat in England.

Moral Treatment at the York Retreat

In 1791, Hannah Mills, a young Quaker woman, died after being admitted to an asylum in York, England (Tuke, 1813/1996). The Quakers believed her death was due to ill treatment at the asylum, so they decided to build their own retreat where those with severe psychological problems could receive care. Under the leadership of William Tuke, the retreat was completed and began operation in 1796. Located in a tranquil rural area near York, England, the retreat consisted of a house surrounded by an 11-acre farm. In the beginning, only members of the Quaker community were admitted as patients, but in time non-Quakers were admitted as well (Tuke, 1813/1996). The retreat, which began with only three patients, had grown to eight by the end of the second year. Eventually, the retreat would care for 70 patients, which required a substantial expansion of its facilities and staff. Some patients worked on the farm, growing vegetables and attending to the animals. Patients had four meals a day, a marked contrast to the starvation rations in public asylums. Tea was formally served each day and patients were invited to dress up and attend. Fresh air was considered important, and patients were allowed to take walks on the retreat grounds. Creative and cultural activities were also considered important and patients were encouraged to read books, read and write poetry, engage in arts and crafts, attend presentations on various topics, and participate in other such activities. In 1797, George Jepson, a man known for his strong character and humane values, became superintendent of the retreat. Jepson later married Katherine Allen, a Quaker nurse who also worked at the retreat. As husband and wife, they created a family-like atmosphere for the patients. The attendants were carefully chosen based on their moral character and their ability to work with patients in a respectful, humane manner. Thus, down to the last detail, the York Retreat was designed to nourish the bodies, minds, and souls of the patients.

The retreat was not, as sometimes depicted, free of medical influence. William Tuke, the retreat's founder, believed it was important to have a physician on staff. Tuke's personal physician, a man named Timothy Maud, filled this role in the beginning. Maud used medical treatments with some of the patients at the retreat. When Maud left, a physician named Thomas Fowler took his place. Fowler also used medical treatments. In his *Description of the Retreat*, Samuel Tuke (1813/1996), the grandson of William Tuke, told how Fowler used bleeding on a manic patient with seemingly favorable results. However, Fowler came to believe that medical treatments were generally unhelpful and often harmful, so he stopped using them except in extreme cases when other methods had failed. Samuel Tuke (1813/1996) praised Fowler for his humility and for his contributions to the retreat in its early days. Glover (1984), a modern scholar on the retreat, was a bit more wry in his praise, saying that "the most creative thing Dr. Fowler did during his short time at the retreat was his courageous abandonment of traditional treatment" (p. 54). After Dr. Fowler died, other physicians worked at the retreat, but it was clear that the social milieu of the retreat, not the occasional medical treatment, was the reason patients improved. Moral treatment was a new and more humane way of working with the insane that stood in marked contrast to the medical treatments offered by physicians.

For almost 25 years (ca. 1799–1823), the York Retreat enjoyed a golden age of success. In the first 15 years of the retreat's operation, 70% of patients admitted in the first year of their illness and 25% of the chronically ill recovered (R. Whitaker, 2002). Most of the patients at the retreat had severe psychological problems. Some had come from hospitals and asylums where they had been considered incurable (Tuke, 1813/1996). Thus, the recovery rates are remarkable. Although the rates may seem hard to believe, recovery rates at future institutions using moral treatment, including facilities in the United States, would be even higher (see the next section).

Moral Treatment in the United States

The success of the York Retreat inspired the establishment of similar retreats and asylums in Europe and the United States. In 1813, the Quakers in Philadelphia established the first asylum in the United States to offer moral treatment. It was called The Asylum for Persons Deprived of the Use of Their Reason, later renamed the Frankford Asylum for the Insane. In the following years, other institutions offering moral treatment were established. These included the Asylum for the Insane, a division of what is now McLean Hospital, which admitted its first patients in 1818; the Bloomingdale Asylum in New York, founded in 1824; the Hartford Retreat in Connecticut, also founded in 1824; the Worcester State Lunatic Hospital in Massachusetts, later renamed the Worcester Hospital, founded in 1833; and the Vermont Asylum for the Insane, later renamed Battleboro Retreat, founded in 1837. These are only a few of the facilities in the United States to offer moral treatment. R. Whitaker (2002) said that "by 1841, there were sixteen private and public asylums in the United States that promised to provide moral treatment to the insane" (p. 25). This figure does not include the asylums and hospitals in Europe that used moral treatment. Thus, moral treatment was a widespread movement that had a major impact on treatment of the insane during the first half of the 1800s.

Grob (1973) and McGovern (1985) reported recovery rates at several U.S. asylums that used moral treatment (also see R. Whitaker, 2002). The Hartford Retreat in Connecticut, which admitted a small number of patients and gave them individualized attention, reported that 21 out of 23 patients (93.3%) recovered during the retreat's first 3 years. Ten years later the recovery rates were still above 90%. In1837, the Worcester Hospital in Massachusetts reported recovery rates of 82%. McLean Hospital, which admitted 732 patients between 1818 and 1830, reported that 59% improved enough to be discharged. The Bloomingdale Asylum in New York, which admitted 1,841 patients between 1821 and 1844, reported that 60% percent were discharged as either "cured" or "improved." Finally, the Quaker asylum in Philadelphia reported regular recovery rates of 50%. It's important to remember that moral treatment was designed for smaller settings where patients could receive individualized attention. The Hartford Retreat, with recovery rates of 90%, was the only setting that followed that principle. Thus, the fact that many patients in large settings also recovered suggests that moral treatment, even in diluted form, had rather potent effects.

The End of Moral Treatment

The success of moral treatment launched an era of optimism that the insane could be cured. Almost everyone, it seemed, was excited about moral treatment. One group, however, was not so excited. Many physicians viewed moral treatment as a threat, for at least two reasons. First, moral treatment showed that humane laypersons could heal the insane better than physicians. Second, it showed that a supportive social environment was more effective than medical treatments. Thus, moral treatment undermined the importance of physicians and limited their ability to profit from the expanding "trade in lunacy" (Parry-Jones, 1972). Physicians were in a dilemma. They could not directly attack moral treatment because they knew it was effective, it was immensely popular with the public, and it was the reason thousands of patients were now seeking treatment. So instead of trying to discredit moral treatment, physicians incorporated it. In 1845, physicians in England lobbied to get the Lunacy Act of 1845 passed (Unsworth, 1993). The law officially changed the status of the insane to patients who required treatment. The act required asylums to be licensed, and to be licensed, a physician had to be in charge. Thus, the Lunacy Act of 1845 put English physicians back in charge of treating the insane. Similar efforts were made in the United States. Physicians and medical societies lobbied state legislatures to pass laws that would place physicians in charge of asylums. In 1844, thirteen medical superintendents of asylums formed the Association of Medical Superintendents of American Institutions for the Insane (AMSAII; the organization would later become the American Psychiatric Association). AMSAII passed a resolution that only physicians could be superintendents of asylums, thus helping to ensure that physicians would hold the power in the "lunacy" field.

In addition to such legal and organizational tactics, physicians also incorporated moral treatment by explaining its effectiveness in biological terms. For example, physicians said that insanity was caused by irritated nerves, and that moral treatment was effective because it provided the rest and relaxation needed for the nerves to recover. Physicians also argued that although moral treatment was effective, it would be even more effective if combined with medical treatments.

As physicians consolidated their power, hospitals and asylums that offered moral treatment increasingly included medical treatments as part of the treatment regimen. In time, moral treatment was marginalized and medical treatments, once again, took center stage. During the second half of the 1800s, recovery rates plummeted, and most asylums and hospitals became little more than warehouses for the insane. Even the York Retreat appointed its first medical superintendent in 1847 and began using medical treatments, including hydrotherapy and drugs. The small, family-like social environment, which had been at the heart of the retreat's success, was left behind as the retreat admitted more patients and took on a medical-like persona (Digby, 1984). By the end of the 1800s, moral treatment, for all practical purposes, had come to an end. The idea that the insane could be cured by kindness and respect was considered a naive view from a bygone era.

Criticisms of Moral Treatment

Moral treatment has had its critics. For example, in the late 1800s, Pliny Earle (1887), a prominent New England psychiatrist, raised concerns about the reported recovery rates of moral treatment. He said that Worcester Hospital, for example, based its success rates on discharges and did not take into account the fact that some patients were readmitted and discharged again, thereby inflating the number of discharges from the hospital. On its surface, Earle's criticism seems to make sense. However, later recalculations showed that taking into account readmissions changed the reported success rate only one quarter of one percent (Warner, 2004). It's also worth noting that Earle was a founder of AMSAII, the association described previously that helped put physicians back in charge of treating the insane. Thus, Earle's criticisms of moral treatment may have been politically motivated. Regardless of his motives, his criticisms appear to have been baseless. Nevertheless, they had an effect and contributed to the demise of moral treatment in the late 1800s.

Perhaps the most extreme criticism of moral treatment came from Michel Foucault (1965), who argued that although moral treatment at the York Retreat was described as a humane approach, it was, in reality, a form of oppressive social control that coerced patients to follow a moral regimen and deprived them of their freedom and rights. Charland (2007), a leading scholar on moral treatment, responded to Foucault's criticisms, saying that benevolence was at the heart of moral treatment and that instead of being an oppressive form of social control, the treatment was, in fact, "fundamentally designed to encourage autonomy, not oppression" (p. 63). Charland said that Foucault's criticisms "appear to be seriously off the mark" (p. 63). Also, Foucault's accusation of oppressive social control falls somewhat flat when one considers that before moral treatment, patients were locked in cells, chained to the walls or floors, controlled by intimidation and violence, and subjected to brutal treatments.

Thus, moral treatment, like any other approach, has been criticized, but most historians and other scholars have concluded that moral treatment was a humane and effective approach that stood in marked contrast to the brutal medical treatments of the day (e.g., Cherry, 1989; Digby,

1985; Glover, 1984; Goodheart, 2003; Hunter & MacAlpine, 1982; Porter, 2002; Scull, 1993; Shorter, 1993, 1997; K. A. Stewart, 1992; Warner, 2004; R. Whitaker, 2002). For purposes of this book, the most important point is that moral treatment demonstrated, for the first time in history, that patients with severe psychological problems could be helped through social means.

Moral Treatment Today

In 1968, Loren Mosher, a Harvard-trained psychiatrist who was teaching at Yale University, was appointed director of the Center for Schizophrenia Studies at the National Institute of Mental Health (NIMH). Mosher became concerned about the overuse of psychiatric drugs and decided to conduct a study to compare treatment of psychotic patients in psychiatric hospitals where drugs were used with an alternative approach that offered patients a home-like setting with psychosocial support. The study began in 1971 with six patients and several staff who lived together in a large house in California. The Soteria Project, as it came to be called, offered a therapeutic milieu that was very similar to that of moral treatment. For example, the project provided a family-like atmosphere, used a nonprofessional staff, provided patients with ongoing emotional and social support, and expected patients to assist with chores and engage in activities designed to support their recovery. Mosher was not opposed to the use of psychiatric drugs in emergencies and for the short term, but the center of treatment was the psychosocial support provided to the Soteria patients. Mosher's findings were quite remarkable (see Bola & Mosher, 2003; Mosher, 1972, 1999; Mosher & Menn, 1977, 1978). They showed that psychotic symptoms of the Soteria patients abated just as quickly as those of patients in psychiatric hospitals taking medication. In addition, the Soteria patients had lower relapse rates and functioned better socially and occupationally. The Soteria Project demonstrated that using social means to help those with severe psychological problems was effective and had advantages over psychiatric hospitalization and drugs. The Soteria Project challenged, at a fundamental level, the way patients with severe psychological problems were treated in the United States. Because of its promise as a viable alternative approach, the Soteria Project was expanded. Then the NIMH cut off its funding and brought the project to an end. Mosher believed the funding was cut because the findings represented a threat to the psychiatric establishment and its ties to the pharmaceutical industry (Bola & Mosher, 2003). Although Soteria came to an end in the United States, Soteria Berne in Switzerland, which was based on Mosher's model, is still in operation, offering patients with severe psychological problems an effective alternative to psychiatric hospitalization and permanent placement on psychiatric drugs (see Ciompi & Hoffman, 2004).

When one looks at the history of socially oriented approaches—whether Pinel's *traitement moral* at the Paris hospitals, moral treatment at the York Retreat, moral treatment in the United States, the Soteria Project in the 1970s, Soteria Berne, or other such projects—a clear picture begins to emerge. Healing through social means works. In fact, it works better than medical treatments. The Soteria Project showed that it works better than hospitalization and psychiatric drugs. In view of this, one has to question why today's psychiatric establishment is so committed to the use of psychiatric drugs, which can have dangerous and sometimes irreversible side effects. What would happen if the billions of dollars that flow into psychiatric hospitals and medications were redirected into building centers that used social means to help those with psychological problems? This is not a rhetorical question, but it's one that deserves attention, especially when the overprescribing of psychiatric drugs has become a national problem.

THE 1900s: BIOLOGICAL TREATMENTS

Once moral treatment had been undermined and physicians were back in charge of the "mental health" field, they turned to biological treatments. Sadly, many of the treatments were as irrational and brutal as those that had been offered in the 1700s. Some of those treatments are described next.

Malarial Therapy

In 1917, Julius Wagner-Jauregg (1857–1940), an Austrian psychiatrist, introduced malarial therapy to treat "general paresis of the insane," a type of insanity associated with late-stage syphilis (Brown, 2000; Tsay, 2013). Wagner-Jauregg had observed that patients with severe psychological problems seemed to improve after having a high fever. So he theorized that inducing a high fever in patients might cure insanity. Wagner-Jauregg inoculated patients with tainted blood from a malarial patient to give them malaria with its attendant high fever. When some of the patients seemed to improve, Wagner-Jauregg concluded that he had discovered an effective treatment for insanity. Others apparently agreed. In 1927, Wagner-Jauregg was awarded the Nobel Prize in Physiology or Medicine (Allerberger, 1997).

Convulsion Therapy

Another biological treatment focused on *dementia praecox*, or schizophrenia. Physicians believed that epilepsy and schizophrenia were mutually antagonistic and theorized that inducing epileptic-like convulsions in patients with schizophrenia might prove curative. In 1933, Manfred Sakel (1994), a psychiatrist in Vienna, used insulin shock therapy for the first time. This was followed in 1934 by the introduction of metrazol shock therapy by Ladislas J. Meduna, a Hungarian psychiatrist (Abrams, 1988; Fink, 1979; Mackay, 1965). In high doses, both insulin and metrazol cause convulsions followed by coma. In 1938, Ugo Cerletti, an Italian neurologist, used electroconvulsive therapy (ECT) for the first time (Shorter, 1997). ECT took precedence over other convulsion treatments and is still being used today (Leiknes, Jarosh-von Schweder, & Høie, 2012).

Psychosurgery

Another biological treatment was psychosurgery. In 1888, Gottlieb Burckhardt, a Swiss psychiatrist, had performed psychosurgery on six patients (H. A. Whitaker, Stemmer, & Joanette, 1996). However, it was Egas Moniz (1874–1955), a Portuguese neurologist, who made psychosurgery a common treatment in the 1900s. Moniz believed that psychological problems, particularly obsessive and depressive problems, were due to a disorder of the synapses that caused the patient's thoughts to follow the same neural circuits continually. He theorized that killing some of the cortical tissue in the prefrontal lobes might break up the pattern and cause the brain to create new neurological pathways (Moniz, 1956). So in 1935, Moniz worked with a surgeon to drill several holes in a patient's skull. They injected ethanol through the holes to kill small areas of the brain in the frontal lobes. After performing several surgeries using ethanol, Moniz decided to cut out small pieces of the brain instead. When some of the patients seemed to improve, Moniz concluded that the treatment was effective.

In the United States, Walter Freeman (1895–1972), a neurologist, and James Watts (1904–1994), a neurosurgeon, were impressed by Moniz's work. However, they thought Moniz's surgery did not go far enough. In their opinion, connections between the prefrontal lobes and deeper structures of the brain should be severed. So they developed a technique that involved drilling a hole in either side of the patient's skull and inserting a sharp instrument to scrape away some of the neural connections between the prefrontal lobes and nearby parts of the brain. Freeman and Watts coined the term *lobotomy* to describe the procedure. Freeman, however, was still not satisfied with the method because it was expensive and required a surgeon, anesthesia, and an operating room. So he modified the procedure. He invented an instrument similar to an ice pick that could be driven into the patient's brain with a hammer. Because the instrument was hammered through the patient's eye socket just above the eye, the procedure did not require a surgeon or an operating room. Freeman believed lobotomies were effective, and he traveled the country in his own van to demonstrate the procedure to other physicians. During his career, Freeman personally performed 3,500 lobotomies. He even performed lobotomies on 19 children; one was only 4 years old (D. G. Stewart & Davis, 2008).

Despite the fact that the procedure posed a significant risk of death and could cause serious and unwanted changes in personality, 5,074 lobotomies were performed in the United States in 1949 (Shorter, 1997; Swayze, 1995). This figure does not include those performed in Europe and other places. Psychosurgery, and especially lobotomy, was considered a major contribution to medicine. To cure psychological problems, simply cut out a piece of the patient's brain or hammer in an ice pick and scramble the neural networks. In 1949, Egas Moniz, the originator of modern psychosurgery, was given the Nobel Prize in Physiology or Medicine for his contributions (Swayze, 1995).

Surgical Removal of Body Parts

Another biological treatment was removal of body parts. The treatment was championed by Henry Andrews Cotton, the medical director of the New Jersey State Hospital at Trenton from 1907 to 1930. Cotton, a psychiatrist, embraced an emerging medical theory that insanity, like many physical illnesses, was caused by infection. Thus, to cure the insane, one had to rid the body of infection by removing body parts that might harbor infection. Cotton began by pulling the patient's teeth. If this did not produce a cure, he next removed the tonsils. If there was still no cure, he removed other organs in succession, including the testicles, ovaries, bladder, spleen, stomach, cervix, and colon. Cotton was convinced that his treatments worked. When he later had a nervous breakdown of his own, he diagnosed his problem as due to infection and had several of his own teeth pulled (Scull, 2005). Eventually, the hospital and Cotton's methods came under criticism, and the New Jersey Senate held investigative hearings. However, eminent physicians, surgeons, and politicians came to Cotton's defense. They said the hospital was the most progressive in the world for treating the insane and that Cotton's theory and methods represented a major advance in medicine (Scull, 2005).

Outside of Cotton's hospital, the body part most commonly removed was the ovaries. Removal of the ovaries in women is equivalent to castration, or removal of the testes, in men. The procedure began in the last quarter of the 1800s and continued into the early 1900s (Braslow, 1996; Thiery, 1998). *Ovariotomy*, the medical term for removal of the ovaries, was based on the misogynist view that women were more emotional than men and that their excessive emotionality was due to the ovaries. Physicians theorized that psychological problems in women were caused or exacerbated by disorders of the ovaries and that removing the ovaries might bring about a cure. Although the procedure began in Europe, Robert Battey, a physician in the United States, made the operation famous by using it extensively and writing about its effectiveness. (e.g., see Battey, 1872, 1876). Thus, the procedure came to be known as Battey's operation. When the general public heard that the operation could cure psychological disorders, thousands of women suffering from emotional problems flocked to physicians to request the operation. Despite the high mortality rate of more than 20% (Dally, 1996; Dowbiggen, 2011), removal of the ovaries "became the fashionable treatment of menstrual madness, neurasthenia, nymphomania, masturbation, and all cases of insanity" (Studd, 2006, p. 411). No one knows how many women, counting those in hospitals and asylums, had their ovaries removed. Edward Shorter (1992), a medical historian at the University of Toronto, said that the treatment is now an embarrassment to the psychiatric profession, and many psychiatric histories exclude any mention of the procedure. Nevertheless, as Shorter wrote, "Battey's operation was not a marginal procedure conducted by a few crackpots, but central in the arsenal of late-nineteenth-century gynecology" (p. 78).

Psychiatric Medications

The development of psychiatric medications is the most influential event in the history of biological treatments. Beginning in the 1950s and extending to the present, psychiatric medications have flooded the market, helping turn the pharmaceutical industry into a multibillion dollar enterprise and further consolidating the power of physicians in the mental health field. Physicians now prescribe drugs for schizophrenia, bipolar disorder, depression, panic, anxiety, obsessive–compulsive disorder, attention-deficit/hyperactivity disorder, posttraumatic stress disorder, alcohol problems, drug problems, sleep problems, stress problems, nicotine problems, obesity problems, and bed-wetting. The American Psychiatric Association revises its *Diagnostic and Statistical Manual of Mental Disorders (DSM)* on a regular basis, always adding new disorders to be treated with psychiatric drugs.

Although most clinicians believe that psychiatric drugs, when properly used, can be helpful, it's alarming that psychiatric drugs, many of which can have serious side effects, are overprescribed and even given to children, some as young as 2 years of age (Coyle, 2000). What makes this even more alarming is that research has shown that in many cases, psychotherapy is just as effective as drugs, does not run the risk of dangerous side effects, and is more resistant to relapse than medications (Hollon, Stewart, & Strunk, 2006; Imel, Malterer, McKay, & Wampold, 2008; Wampold, 2010). Concerns about psychiatric drugs have been raised by a wide range of professionals. R. Whitaker (2002) pointed out that individuals who develop psychosis in technologically less advanced countries, where psychiatric medications are not used, are far more likely to recover than similar patients in the United States who are given antipsychotic drugs.

Is it possible that our psychiatric system, which is based on a biological model and the use of psychiatric drugs, is part of the problem instead of the solution? Do we need a new system that, without rejecting the biological model or the appropriate use of drugs, would place human connection and social interaction at the center of the system? The history of medical treatments described in this chapter should give us pause. The medical establishment does not have an admirable historical record when it comes to treatment of the insane. It is possible that today's drug-dominated treatments are yet another problem created by the psychiatric system. I realize, of course, that the psychiatric system in the United States—which includes hundreds of hospitals, all of the major pharmaceutical companies, and 40,000 psychiatrists who treat several million patients—has no interest in changing. Nevertheless, when one considers the growing problems created by psychiatric drugs, including the fact that even preschool children are now being given antipsychotic medications, one has to think that many patients, even today, need to be liberated from their chains and offered more humane treatment.

95

CONCLUSION

As this chapter shows, moral treatment was little more than a brief interlude in the history of treatments that were often more brutal than curative. Moral treatment stands out as an example of a humane and effective approach that used social means to help those with severe psychological problems. Perhaps the most important lesson to be learned from moral treatment is that kindness, caring, and respect are powerful factors in emotional healing. What Pinel and Tuke discovered more than 200 years ago has been confirmed by contemporary research: Human connection and social interaction are potent factors in emotional healing. Thus, this chapter lays another foundation stone for a nonmedical model of psychotherapy.

5

Summary of the Model and Implications for Clinical Research, Training, and Practice

Since the beginning of our profession, the medical model of psychotherapy has shaped clinical research, training, and practice. Freud and other pioneers, in line with medical-model thinking, believed their theories and techniques were responsible for therapeutic effectiveness; they presented research primarily in the form of case studies in an effort to demonstrate that effectiveness; and they trained others in their theories and techniques. Today, not much has changed in that regard. Most clinicians still believe theories and techniques are responsible for effectiveness; researchers still publish studies in an effort to demonstrate that effectiveness; and training programs, including practicum and internship settings, still place heavy emphasis on theories and techniques. In short, the medical model continues to dictate how clinical research, training, and practice are conducted. Thus, it would be naive to present a nonmedical model

http://dx.doi.org/10.1037/14751-006
The Human Elements of Psychotherapy: A Nonmedical Model of Emotional Healing, by D. N. Elkins

without also discussing the challenges of implementing the model in a profession still dominated by medical-model thinking.

In line with this perspective, this chapter presents a brief summary of the nonmedical model and an explanation of how it differs from other common factors models. Then, the chapter describes the model's implications for clinical research, training, and practice along with the obstacles that make it difficult to implement these new directions.

COMMON FACTORS MODELS

Other models based on a common factors perspective have also been developed (see, e.g., Anderson, Lunnen, & Ogles, 2010; Frank & Frank, 1991; Garfield, 1992; Lambert, 1992; Lambert & Ogle, 2004). One of the best-known models is Lambert's (1986, 1992) pie chart, which identified the major therapeutic factors and the percentage each contributed to outcome. Although Lambert's chart was not intended to be a model of psychotherapy, it has implications for psychotherapy. Lambert's model helped launch the common factors movement (see Chapter 1 for more information on Lambert).

Another well-known model is Jerome Frank's common features model. As discussed in Chapter 1, Frank (Frank & Frank, 1991, pp. 38–44) identified four features that are common to all therapies: (a) an emotionally charged, confiding relationship with a helping person; (b) a healing setting; (c) a rationale, conceptual scheme, or myth that provides a plausible explanation for the client's symptoms and prescribes a ritual or procedure for resolving them; and (d) a ritual or procedure that requires the active participation of both patient and therapist and is believed by both to be the means of restoring the patient's health. Frank believed these four common features, instead of specific treatments, were responsible for therapeutic outcome.

More recently, Anderson et al. (2010) proposed a model based on Frank's common features. The authors wanted to avoid the "techniques versus common factors" divide, so they placed treatments at the center of their model and then used Frank's common features for the theoretical structure. They did this to emphasize that treatments contribute to effectiveness in their role as common factors and provide structure for the delivery of other therapeutic factors. As the authors put it, "Without a treatment, the factors, like techniques, are simply ingredients; with a treatment, they form a coherent and viable package of what is known as psychotherapy" (p. 145). In contrast, my model relegates treatments to the margins and places common factors, and particularly human factors, at the center. I believe this reflects the evidence and avoids privileging models and techniques, even as common factors.

All of the models based on a common factors perspective have made important contributions to our profession. I believe the model presented in this book will be useful because it incorporates findings on emotional healing from diverse disciplines and places the potent human elements at the center of psychotherapy. To my knowledge, no other model has done this.

SUMMARY OF THIS BOOK'S NONMEDICAL MODEL

The nonmedical model presented in this book places the human elements at the center. It consists of the following principles, which are supported by evidence summarized in the previous chapters:

- *Humans are evolved to develop, maintain, and restore their emotional well-being through supportive relationships with others.* This principle is based on the evidence from attachment theory and social relationships research that as infants and children we *develop* emotional well-being through relationships, and as adults we *maintain* and *restore* emotional well-being through relationships. The principle underscores the importance of human connection and social interaction and their powerful effects on emotional well-being.
- *Humans are evolved with the ability to give and receive emotional healing through social means.* This principle is based on findings from neuroscience and evolutionary theory that our brains evolved in a social context with the ability to interact through social means with other brains

in the interest of emotional healing. Emotional healing is ubiquitous in the human species. We engage in giving and receiving emotional healing through social means as part of life.

■ *Psychotherapy is an expression of our evolutionarily derived ability to give and receive emotional healing through social means.* This principle affirms that psychotherapy is a subset of our ability to heal one another emotionally through social means. Psychotherapy harnesses the power of our evolutionarily derived ability to heal through social means and uses it to restore the client's emotional well-being. This is not to equate psychotherapy with common, everyday relationships but, rather, to emphasize that psychotherapy is cut from the same cloth.

■ *Psychotherapy changes the client's brain and restores the client's emotional well-being.* This principle is based on evidence from neuroscience that psychotherapy is a brain-altering process. The human brain evolved in a social context with the remarkable ability to change in response to social experience. Thus, psychotherapy can be conceptualized as an intense social experience that changes the client's brain. Old neural circuits are modified and new circuits are created. From a neurobiological perspective, this is how psychotherapy heals.

■ *Psychotherapy heals primarily through social means, not through medical-like techniques.* This principle points to a major distinction between the medical model and the nonmedical model. Whereas the medical model assumes that psychotherapy heals primarily through modalities and techniques, the nonmedical model assumes that psychotherapy heals primarily through social means, or what this book calls the *human elements.* In other words, psychotherapy heals through human connection and social interaction. It's an interpersonal process, not a medical procedure.

■ *Common factors, and particularly human factors, are the most potent determinants of effectiveness in psychotherapy, dwarfing the effects of modalities and techniques.* This principle is the cornerstone of the nonmedical model of psychotherapy. It is based on the compelling evidence from clinical research that specific modalities and techniques have relatively little to do with therapeutic effectiveness, whereas

Table 5.1

Contrasting Models of Psychotherapy

Medical model	Nonmedical model
Modalities and techniques are the agents of change.	Common factors, particularly human factors, are the agents of change.
Psychotherapy is a medical-like procedure.	Psychotherapy is an interpersonal process.
Psychotherapy heals through techniques.	Psychotherapy heals through social means.
Psychotherapy is grounded in medicine.	Psychotherapy is grounded in the relationship sciences.
The therapist is the expert on what the client needs.	The client is the expert on what the client needs.
The therapist's role is to administer techniques.	The therapist's role is to create a healing situation.
The client's role is to follow the therapist's instructions.	The client's role is to give the therapist instructions.
The therapeutic relationship facilitates the treatment.	The therapeutic relationship is the treatment.
Cannot explain why all psychotherapies are effective	Can explain why all psychotherapies are effective
Is not supported by contemporary science	Is supported by contemporary science

common factors, and particularly human factors, are major determinants of effectiveness. The principle shows why we need a nonmedical model of psychotherapy that places the human elements at the center of therapeutic work.

Table 5.1 summarizes the differences between this nonmedical model and the prevailing medical model of psychotherapy. It is important to note that the nonmedical model does not eliminate modalities and techniques. Although they have little inherent power to heal, modalities and techniques do contribute to outcome in their role as common factors that provide structure for the therapeutic work and serve as conduits for other therapeutic factors. Thus, modalities and techniques have a role to play in the nonmedical model, but they are less important than the common factors.

IMPLICATIONS FOR CLINICAL RESEARCH

The implications of the nonmedical model for clinical research are that clinical scientists need to reduce the amount of research focused on modalities and techniques and increase the amount focused on common factors, and especially human factors. This section discusses these implications in the context of the challenges that make their implementation difficult.

Ignoring the Evidence

One of the biggest challenges is that some clinical scientists continue to ignore the evidence that common factors, and particularly human factors, are the primary determinants of effectiveness in psychotherapy (see, e.g., Baker, McFall, & Shoham, 2009). This is puzzling. Why would scientists ignore evidence? I think some were caught in the "technique zeitgeist" that began in the 1970s when the health insurance industry began pressuring psychologists to use "scientifically validated" techniques. For several decades, scientists conducted research and published articles that described various techniques as empirically supported. However, beginning in the late 1990s, Wampold and his associates conducted meta-analyses of hundreds of published studies that showed that so-called empirically supported treatments were no more effective than other treatments (see Chapter 1, this volume). Thus, the long search for specific techniques to heal specific disorders was a failure. Elkins (2012a) described the extent of that failure:

> Thus, after 40 years of specificity research and millions of research dollars, there is still no scientific basis for privileging one modality and set of techniques over other modalities and techniques. Instead, scientific findings confirm that all bona fide psychotherapies are robustly effective, and equally so. (p. 451)

Specificity research did make one important contribution: It showed us what *doesn't* work in psychotherapy and opened the door to new ideas about emotional healing. Fortunately, during the years that clinical scientists were searching for "silver bullet" techniques, scientists in other disciplines were making discoveries that would change our understanding of emotional healing and how it occurs. Unknown at the time, a perfect storm was brewing as three major "weather systems" began to converge: (a) the search for specific techniques to heal specific disorders would come up empty; (b) meta-analyses of hundreds of published studies would show that common factors, not techniques, are the major determinants of effectiveness; and (c) discoveries in other disciplines would provide a new understanding of emotional healing. Today, we are in the midst of that perfect storm, and it's changing our profession. Unfortunately, some clinical scientists have dedicated years to specificity research. Their articles and books, along with their professional reputations, reflect that work. So it's difficult to let go of the dream of finding silver bullet techniques and to acknowledge that, for all those years, they were focusing on the wrong factors in their research. Nevertheless, the evidence is now overwhelming that psychotherapy's robust effectiveness is due primarily to common factors, and particularly human factors. So it's time for all clinical scientists to embrace the evidence, as painful as doing so may be, and begin to focus research on the factors in therapy that are responsible for its effectiveness.

Hard Science Attitudes

Another obstacle is "hard science" attitudes. Perhaps due to their hard science training, some scientists find it difficult to believe that such "soft" factors as empathy, caring, and support could be responsible for effectiveness. Bohart commented on this problem: "How often do you hear scientists use language such as 'hard science,' 'tough-minded,' 'unsentimental,' 'ruthless, cold logic' and 'no nonsense' as if they take pride in being hard and unsentimental" (A. Bohart, personal communication, April 24, 2007). Techniques "fit" hard science attitudes; the two go hand-in-hand. Techniques can be operationally defined; they can be described in objective, behavioral terms; and they can be administered in a standardized way. In contrast, the human elements of psychotherapy are difficult to define operationally; hard to describe in objective, behavioral terms; and can't be administered in a standardized way. There's no protocol for empathy, caring, and support. In fact, it would seem strange to speak of administering these elements. Thus, techniques are appealing to a certain kind of scientific mind, whereas the human elements are not appealing. The only problem, of course, is that we now know that techniques have little to do with effectiveness, whereas the human elements are potent determinants of effectiveness. Thus, scientists with hard science attitudes need to broaden their philosophy of science and begin to conduct research on these soft but powerful elements of emotional healing.

Of course, clinical scientists are not the only ones who like techniques. Our entire profession seems enamored with them. Why is this so? I believe it's due to the medical-model thinking that still dominates our profession. From the beginning, the medical model led us to believe that if techniques work in medicine, they will work in psychotherapy. Until recently, that belief was never seriously challenged. Today, it's being challenged. As a result, we are finally realizing that medical healing and emotional healing are different, and just because techniques work in medicine does not mean they work in psychotherapy. Techniques work in medicine because human bodies are all essentially the same, regardless of the patient's ethnicity, culture, and life experiences. If administering an antibiotic cures pneumonia in one patient, it is likely to cure pneumonia in another patient. If an appendectomy cures appendicitis in one patient, it will cure appendicitis in another patient. Thus, medical healing can be organized into standardized techniques because human bodies are standardized, meaning they are all essentially the same. However, this is not true of emotional healing. Standardized techniques don't work in psychotherapy because each client's emotional make-up is different, formed by a diverse and interacting array of genetic, biological, personal, familial, societal, and cultural factors. Even clients with the same psychological problem, such as clinical depression, differ widely in their emotional make-up and in the way they experience and express their depression. Thus, emotional healing, unlike medical healing, cannot be organized into standardized protocols. Instead, psychotherapists must tailor their approach to the unique emotional makeup of each client and even to the client's changing thoughts, emotions, and behaviors as the therapy proceeds. This is why the personal qualities and interpersonal abilities of therapists are so important. Almost anyone can learn to administer a standardized technique, but it takes an "artist of the soul" to know exactly when and how to extend empathy, care, and support. Physicians may be able to view their patients as biological "mechanisms" that can be "fixed" with mechanistic techniques, but psychotherapists do not have this luxury. We cannot think of our clients as mechanisms, and we cannot fix their emotional pain with mechanistic techniques.

Theoretical Allegiances

Another obstacle to implementing the nonmedical model is that many clinical scientists have allegiance to a particular system of psychotherapy. Thus, they have vested interests, including financial interests, in the outcome of studies they conduct. Is this a conflict of interest that should be avoided? I am not suggesting that clinical scientists are dishonest or that they would intentionally skew results. I am suggesting, however, that scientists who have vested interests, including financial interests, in the outcome of studies may not be the best ones to conduct those studies. Researcher bias can affect studies even when those conducting the studies believe they are being completely objective. An even more basic question is this: Why do clinical scientists continue to conduct studies on the efficacy of specific modalities and techniques? If all therapies are effective and equally so, then why should scientists continue to pit one therapeutic system against others? Perhaps it's time for clinical scientists to rise above the "battle of the brands" and adopt a common focus in research on the factors in all therapies that are primarily responsible for change. As I said elsewhere (Elkins, 2012a),

> A common focus . . . would mean that clinical scientists would reject theoretical allegiances and refuse to use their scientific abilities in the service of a particular system. In other words, a common focus in research means that researchers would transcend schismatic allegiances and work collaboratively to understand the common determinants of effectiveness found in all bona fide therapies. (p. 452)

A Research Scenario

Another problem, closely related to the one just mentioned, is the *way* psychotherapy research is often conducted. Consider the following scenario: A clinician develops a new treatment and designs a study to compare the treatment with an existing treatment. Clients are randomly assigned to receive either the new treatment or the old treatment. One group of therapists administers the new treatment; another group administers the old treatment. When the study is completed and the results are analyzed, the new treatment is found to be more effective than the old treatment. Encouraged by the results, the clinician conducts a second study using more clients. Once again, the results show that the new treatment is more effective than the old treatment. The clinician publishes the studies and describes the new treatment as evidence based and more effective than the existing treatment.

This scenario is common, and many see nothing wrong with it. However, let's continue the scenario. A scientist decides to take a closer look at the research and discovers two problems. First, the clinician who conducted the studies assumed that the treatments, meaning the modalities and techniques, were responsible for outcome. Closer analysis, however, shows that common factors were the major determinants of outcome and that modalities and techniques had little effect. Second, the clinician who conducted the studies failed to take into account the effects of therapist allegiance. The scientist discovers that all the therapists were colleagues of the clinician and had even contributed to the development of the new treatment. Thus, they "believed in" the efficacy of the new treatment. They had "allegiance" to it. Although the therapists who administered the old treatment had undergone training to help ensure that they administered it correctly, their allegiance was actually to the new treatment. They had no allegiance to the treatment they administered in the studies. Because therapist allegiance can account for as much as 10% of the outcome variance, the scientist decides to reanalyze the data taking into account therapist allegiance. The reanalysis shows that the new treatment was no more effective than the old treatment. Its apparent "edge" over the old treatment was due entirely to the effects of therapist allegiance.

The first part of the previous scenario occurs too often, and the second part does not occur often enough. This is one reason that we have a constant stream of new books and workshops on the latest evidence-based treatments. Before buying the books and attending the workshops, we should ask at least two questions about the research: (a) Were the data analyzed to determine whether common factors, not the treatment itself, could have been responsible for the outcome? and (b) Were other factors known to affect outcome (e.g., therapist allegiance in the scenario) taken into account in the design and data analysis? If the answers to these questions are not satisfactory, then we should not buy the books or attend the workshops. It's likely that the Dodo bird is lurking in the data and that the new treatment is no more effective than the treatment we are currently using.

Research Funding Agencies

Perhaps the biggest obstacle to implementing the implications of the non-medical model in clinical research is that most research funding agencies continue to embrace the medical model of psychotherapy. This makes it almost impossible to secure funding for psychotherapy research without casting the application in medical-model language and focusing the study on the efficacy of specific treatments. Thus, there's a strong economic incentive for clinical scientists to design research projects that focus on modalities and techniques and little economic incentive to design projects that focus on the common factors, including the human factors. In other words, the economic tail wags the research-design dog. If this is to change, funding agencies will have to moderate their attachment to the medical model and fund more projects on the factors in psychotherapy that are primarily responsible for effectiveness. As long as funding agencies embrace the medical model, studies on modalities and techniques will continue to proliferate, and studies on the common factors, including the human factors, will be limited.

New Territory for Research

Despite the obstacles in the field of clinical research, the human elements of psychotherapy represent new opportunities for important research.

The evidence shows that the human elements are potent determinants of effectiveness, but we know relatively little about them and how they operate in therapy. For example, we know that therapists have significant effects on therapeutic outcome, yet we have relatively little information on how highly effective therapists conduct therapy (Duncan, Miller, Wampold, & Hubble, 2010). We also need studies on how the human elements heal in therapy and how therapists can support, activate, and perhaps even amplify their effects. Thus, the human elements of psychotherapy represent a vast new territory for clinical research.

IMPLICATIONS FOR CLINICAL TRAINING

The nonmedical model also has important implications for clinical training. Generally, the implications are that training programs need to reduce the focus on modalities and techniques and increase the focus on the human elements of psychotherapy. However, this is easier said than done. Like the field of clinical research, the field of clinical training is dominated by the medical model. Thus, academic courses, along with practicum and internship training, are based on medical-model assumptions, and this culture will not change easily. However, because training programs want to produce the best clinicians possible, there is reason to believe that, in time, training will move in more progressive directions. In the meantime, for programs that already understand the importance of a nonmedical approach, perhaps the following suggestions will prove helpful.

Student Selection

One implication of the nonmedical model is that training programs need to select students who have the personal qualities and interpersonal abilities to become effective healers. Currently, most programs select students on the basis of their intellectual and academic abilities and pay little attention to personal and interpersonal qualities. As Peter Breggin (1991) wrote,

> Training programs for psychotherapists . . . are not even trying to screen their applicants to find good, kind people who will become

loving and understanding therapists. They are competing with other programs for the students with the highest test scores, the best college grades, and the most impressive academic recommendations. (p. 406)

This needs to change because we now know that therapists are potent determinants of effectiveness in psychotherapy and their potency has a great deal to do with their personal qualities and interpersonal abilities. This does not mean that we should deemphasize students' intellectual and academic abilities. Instead, it means that we should emphasize their personal and interpersonal qualities more than is currently the case. As Norcross (2010) said, "We must select students for graduate training who are both academically qualified and interpersonally skilled" (p. 134). Being bright and being kind are not mutually exclusive; academic abilities and caring are not antagonistic qualities. In the large population of those who apply for graduate training in psychotherapy, there is a subpopulation of applicants who are both exceptionally bright and also unusually kind, caring, and empathic. If programs want to select the "best of the best," then they should select students from this subpopulation.

How, specifically, can this be done? First, a training program might state in its catalog and other informational materials that the program places special emphasis on the personal and interpersonal qualities of applicants. Second, the program might ask those who write letters of recommendation to address in detail the personal and interpersonal qualities of applicants. Third, if an applicant appears to be qualified, a representative of the program could contact references to discuss in more depth the applicant's personal and interpersonal qualities. Fourth, programs could conduct face-to-face interviews with top applicants to observe and evaluate firsthand their personal and interpersonal qualities. Fifth, the program could invite top applicants to visit the campus on a day set aside for this purpose. The applicants would interact with administrators, faculty, staff, current students, and other applicants while on campus. It's likely that those who are kind, caring, and empathic will stand out.

Of course, this is new territory and these are only suggestions. Training programs may find other and better ways to select students who have the qualities to become effective healers. Nevertheless, I believe these concrete suggestions show that if a program wants to select such students, it can be done.

Academic Training

Academic training refers to courses and other educational activities that are designed to increase students' knowledge. Unfortunately, academic training in most programs is shaped by the medical model. For example, students are expected to use medical language when discussing psychotherapy; they are required to learn about pathology, diagnosis, and treatment. At the same time, little emphasis is placed on developing the qualities associated with being an effective emotional healer. It seems we are trying to produce "junior physicians" instead of psychotherapists. Thus, one strong implication of the nonmedical model for academic training is that we need to stop training junior physicians and begin training psychotherapists.

How, practically, can this be done? First, training programs could offer a course early in the program on the determinants of effectiveness in psychotherapy. Such a course would provide students with an orientation on how psychotherapy heals and help them develop their clinical abilities with this in mind. Second, current academic courses could be modified to reflect the orientation described previously. In other words, all courses need to reflect the fact that the human elements are the most potent determinants of effectiveness and that techniques have relatively little to do with effectiveness. Third, professors who teach courses on psychotherapy should provide a metatheoretical perspective that recognizes the value and effectiveness of all therapeutic systems. In other words, professors should not tell students that some modalities and techniques are more effective than others. Instead, professors should tell students that all bona fide therapies are effective and encourage them to learn various approaches so they can tailor their approach to the client's needs. Fourth, new courses should be added to the curriculum. For example, programs might offer a course on case conceptualization from a nonmedical model perspective and a course on how to support and activate the human elements of psychotherapy.

Supervised Clinical Experience

Supervised clinical experience refers to students' hands-on experience of working with clients under supervision of an experienced clinician. Most training programs require several hundred hours of practicum and a predoctoral internship of 1,500 to 2,000 hours. In addition, many states require a postdoctoral internship for licensure. Thus, supervised clinical experience is a huge component of clinical training. Unfortunately, clinical supervisors often spend a great deal of time discussing diagnosis, treatment planning, and techniques and relatively little time discussing the importance of developing a caring relationship with clients. Thus, one implication of the nonmedical model is that clinical supervisors need to focus more time on the human and relational aspects of therapy. This does not mean that supervisors should ignore diagnosis, treatment planning, and techniques but, rather, that they should focus more time on the factors that are primarily responsible for client change.

Cultivating Students' Personal Qualities and Interpersonal Abilities

If human connection and social interaction are the most potent agents of emotional healing, then training programs should help students to cultivate their personal qualities and interpersonal abilities so that they can connect and interact with clients in an effective way. How can this be done? Training programs could require students to have personal psychotherapy. Frieda Fromm-Reichmann (1950) noted that trying to be a therapist without first being a client "is fraught with danger, hence unacceptable" (p. 42). Would personal therapy be beneficial to students? In a survey conducted by Pope and Tabachnik (1994), the researchers asked clinicians who had been in therapy if it had been beneficial and, if so, to name the most important benefit. Of the 399 clinicians who responded, 86% said their therapy had been "very helpful" or "exceptionally helpful." (Only two respondents said their therapy had not been helpful at all.) The most important benefit named by the most respondents was "self-awareness or self-understanding"; the second was "self-esteem or self-confidence"; and the third was "improved skills as a therapist."

More recently, Norcross (2010) summarized two studies (Bike, Norcross, & Schatz, 2009; Norcross, Dryden, & DeMichele, 1992) in which more than 1,400 psychologists were asked to name what they had learned from their personal therapy regarding the practice of psychotherapy. Summarizing the responses, Norcross (2010) wrote,

> The most frequent responses all involved the interpersonal relation-ships and dynamics of psychotherapy: the centrality of warmth, empa-thy, and the personal relationship; the importance of transference and countertransference; the inevitable humanness of the therapist; and the need for therapist reliability and commitment. (p. 116)

Thus, clinicians who have personal therapy believe it is beneficial to them both personally and professionally. If students were required to have therapy as part of their training, I suspect they would find it highly ben-eficial also.

Experiential Learning

In addition to requiring personal therapy, training programs might also require students to participate in activities and experiences that are spe-cifically designed to increase personal growth and interpersonal skills. For example, programs could offer an ongoing psychoeducational group expe-rience focused specifically on cultivating the personal qualities and inter-personal skills associated with being effective therapists. Unfortunately, in many training programs, such "experiential learning" is marginalized or nonexistent. This needs to change. Experiential learning offers students something that traditional academic courses cannot. Students cannot learn how to listen empathically simply by hearing a lecture on empathy; they cannot learn how to handle confrontation simply by reading a book; they cannot learn that they come across to others as "distant" without honest feedback from others. Training programs must realize that students cannot become effective healers simply by reading books and listening to lectures. If human connection and social interaction are at the core of effective therapy, then programs need to offer activities and experiences specifically designed to cultivate and enhance students' qualities and abilities in those areas.

Emphasis on the Personal

Closely related to the previous suggestions, I believe programs need to place more emphasis on the personal. By "the personal" I mean heartfelt emotions and students' life experiences. There seems to be an unwritten rule in graduate education that personal sharing by students and professors is not appropriate. If we were training engineers or mathematicians, this might make sense. However, we are training therapists whose "subject matter" will be the heartfelt emotions and personal life experiences of their clients. Thus, it seems to me that students could learn a lot about this subject matter by speaking heart-to-heart with one another and their professors. To put it another way, I believe the ambiance or "milieu" of training programs should be personal and human in tone. I am not suggesting that "the personal" should replace academic learning. Instead, I'm suggesting that the personal should be welcome, even encouraged. As a professor who has trained clinicians for 30 years, I am convinced that students learn best when they feel free to share their personal emotions and experiences in class. Personal sharing does not detract from academic learning; it enriches it.

IMPLICATIONS FOR CLINICAL PRACTICE

The nonmedical model of psychotherapy also has implications for clinical practice. The general implication is that clinicians should focus less on modalities and techniques and more on connecting and interacting with clients in a caring, empathic manner. At a basic level, they should think of themselves as emotional healers and "artists of the soul"—not as junior physicians wielding medical-like techniques. In this section I discuss this implication in more specific and practical terms.

Building a Strong Therapeutic Alliance

Perhaps the most important implication of the nonmedical model for clinical practice is that therapists need to build a strong alliance with their clients. The nonmedical model posits that emotional healing occurs primarily through the human connection and social interaction of client and therapist. Thus, the nature and quality of the therapeutic alliance are extremely important as hundreds of studies confirm (Norcross, 2010). How can we build a strong alliance with our clients? More than 50 years ago, C. Rogers (1957) published a seminal article on the necessary and sufficient conditions for therapeutic change. The conditions included (a) empathic understanding of the client's internal frame of reference, (b) unconditional positive regard, and (c) therapist congruence. Over the past 50 years, a great deal of research has been conducted on those three factors. A summary of that research showed that empathy, positive regard, and congruence are essential features of effective therapy and effective therapists (Norcross, 2010). Thus, to build a strong therapeutic alliance, there's no better place to begin than with empathy, positive regard, and congruence.

Tailoring Therapy to Each Client's Needs

Because client factors are the most potent determinants of therapeutic outcome, therapists should do everything possible to support and activate the client's own self-righting capabilities. This would include collaborating with the client to choose a therapeutic approach that fits the client's personal and cultural needs, gathering routine feedback from the client about what is working and not working in the therapy, and supporting the client's involvement in relationships and activities that the client finds to be growthful and healing.

Encouraging Clients to Engage in Extratherapeutic Relationships and Activities

Another implication of the nonmedical model is that clinicians should encourage clients to engage in growth-promoting relationships and activities outside of therapy. Extratherapeutic factors, meaning what happens to clients outside of therapy, have a significant effect on therapeutic outcome. We know that social relationships can have powerful effects on emotional well-being, so it makes sense to encourage clients to engage in relationships with friends or family members who are especially caring, empathic, and supportive. Also, moral treatment, which was discussed in Chapter 4, emphasized the importance of engaging in activities that nourish emotional well-being. Fortunately, therapists can influence extratherapeutic factors so that clients have outside sources of healing and support in addition to the psychotherapy itself.

Gathering and Using Client Feedback

Another implication of the nonmedical model is that clinicians should gather and use client feedback on a regular basis to ensure that the therapy is working effectively for the client. One of the changes that has occurred in the practice of psychotherapy is the privileging of the client's perspective. The traditional model of the therapist as expert who "knows best" and the client as passive recipient of treatment is being replaced by a model that views the client as an active partner in therapy who knows, better than the therapist, what is working and not working. Client factors, which are part of the common factors in therapy, have potent effects on outcome (see Chapter 1). Thus, privileging the client, which means placing the client at the center of psychotherapy, is now considered an important part of conducting effective therapy (Duncan et al., 2010). One of the best ways to privilege the client is to gather and use client feedback. Studies by Duncan (2014) and Lambert (2010a, 2010b) have shown that gathering and using client feedback dramatically increases therapeutic effectiveness and reduces client drop-out rates. Duncan (2014) believes the best way to become a better therapist is to solicit client feedback at every session. He developed Partners for Change Outcome Management System, a client feedback system that helps therapists to gather and use client feedback in an effective way (see Chapter 1 for more details).

Emphasizing the Therapist's Personal Growth

Another implication of the nonmedical model is that therapists should pursue their own personal growth. If the human elements of psychotherapy are the major determinants of effectiveness, then therapists need to focus on their personal and interpersonal development, striving to become the most caring, empathic, and genuine person possible, knowing that the more they grow and the more interpersonally sensitive they become, the better therapist—and human being—they will be. How, in practical terms, can this be done? First, therapists should try to surround themselves with friends and colleagues who are also dedicated to personal growth. Unfortunately, some professionals have no interest in taking the interpersonal risks necessary to grow personally. To the degree possible, such colleagues should be avoided in favor of those who are open, self-disclosing, and genuinely committed to personal and interpersonal growth. Second, therapists should consider taking workshops and continuing education courses that focus on personal and interpersonal development. Third, special emphasis should be placed on developing the personal qualities and interpersonal skills that promote therapeutic effectiveness. In 2002, a committee of American Psychological Association Division 29, Psychotherapy, chaired by John Norcross (2002) conducted a review of the research to identify relational factors that contribute to effectiveness in psychotherapy. On the basis of the amount and quality of the evidence supporting particular factors, the committee categorized factors as either "demonstrably effective" or "promising and probably effective" (see Steering Committee, 2002). Three relational factors were placed in the first category of demonstrably effective: therapist's level of empathy, quality of the therapeutic alliance, and level of agreement between client and therapist on the goals of therapy. Seven factors were placed in the second category of promising and probably effective: positive regard, congruence, quality of the therapist's feedback, frequency and quality of the therapist's self-disclosure, the therapist's willingness to address and repair ruptures in the relationship, management of countertransference, and quality of the therapist's interpretations. These relational factors provide a blueprint for therapists who want to grow in ways that are likely to increase their therapeutic effectiveness.

Understanding the Role of Modalities and Techniques

Another implication of the nonmedical model is that clinicians need to understand the role of modalities and techniques in psychotherapy. Modalities and techniques serve three main purposes in psychotherapy. First, they provide structure for the therapeutic work. Second, in their role as common factors, they contribute to therapeutic outcome. Third, they serve as a conduit or means for the delivery of other therapeutic factors. I believe therapists who understand this are in a better position to be more effective. For example, they can relinquish adherence to a particular theory and techniques and use any approach that fits the client's needs. Also, they can spend less time memorizing treatment protocols and more time focusing on how to create a therapeutic relationship characterized by caring, empathy, acceptance, and support. In short, they can stop focusing on things that make little difference and begin focusing on the factors in psychotherapy that really matter.

CONCLUSION

Fortunately, thousands of clinicians have already adopted a nonmedical approach in their therapeutic work. They have learned from clinical experience that the human and relational elements are the center of psychotherapy, that the client's emotional pain can only be healed by someone who genuinely cares. For these clinicians, this book will simply give scientific confirmation of what they have already learned and what they practice every day.

By presenting a nonmedical model and its implications for research, training, and practice, this chapter has provided a blueprint for change. However, if change is to occur, it will likely be due to a groundswell of professionals who understand the evidence and begin to make changes in their professional work. If you are a clinical researcher, I urge you to focus some of your research efforts on the human elements of psychotherapy; if you are a professor in a clinical training program, I hope you will discuss the evidence for common factors with your students; and if you are a psychotherapist who has focused on modalities and techniques, I hope you will focus more attention on the human elements. On the other hand, if you are among the thousands of clinicians who already know from personal experience that the human and relational elements are the primary agents of healing, then continue to do what you've been doing and know that science is on your side.

Afterword

We are in the midst of one of the greatest revolutions in the history of psychotherapy. The old paradigm has been undermined, and a new paradigm is struggling to be born. Paradigms change slowly, and those committed to the old paradigm do not yield easily. Nevertheless, there are reasons to believe that the new paradigm will eventually prevail. First, the evidence supports the new paradigm; it does not support the old one. Second, change is already occurring as increasing numbers of clinicians, scientists, students, and others are realizing that common factors, not modalities and techniques, are the major determinants of effectiveness in psychotherapy. Third, the history of science is filled with discoveries that undermined old paradigms and created new ones. Those who were devoted to the old paradigm always resisted the new one. Nevertheless, the new paradigm, if supported by the evidence, eventually prevailed. This history gives reason to hope that, in time, the medical model of psychotherapy will be abandoned and a more human and relational model will be adopted. I believe that those who embrace the new model will be on the right side of history and will have opportunities to make new and exciting contributions to the field of psychotherapy.

I hope this book contributes to the revolution. I hope it helps build the new paradigm.

http://dx.doi.org/10.1037/14751-007
The Human Elements of Psychotherapy: A Nonmedical Model of Emotional Healing, by D. N. Elkins

References

Abrams, R. (1988). *Electroconvulsive therapy.* Oxford, England: Oxford University Press.

Ahn, H., & Wampold, B. E. (2001). Where oh where are the specific ingredients? A meta-analysis of component studies in counseling and psychotherapy. *Journal of Counseling Psychology, 48,* 251–257. http://dx.doi.org/10.1037/0022-0167.48.3.251

Ainsworth, M. (1967). *Infancy in Uganda: Infant care and the growth of love.* Baltimore, MD: Johns Hopkins University Press.

Ainsworth, M. D. (1969). Object relations, dependency, and attachment: A theoretical review of the infant–mother relationship. *Child Development, 40,* 969–1025. http://dx.doi.org/10.2307/1127008

Ainsworth, M. (1991). Attachments and other affectional bonds across the life cycle. In C. M. Parkes, J. Stevenson-Hinde, & P. Marris (Eds.), *Attachment across the life cycle* (pp. 33–51). London, England: Routledge.

Ainsworth, M., Blehar, M., Waters, E., & Wall, S. (Eds.). (1978). *Patterns of attachment: A psychological study of the Strange Situation.* Hillsdale, NJ: Erlbaum.

Ainsworth, M., & Bowlby, J. (1991). An ethological approach to personality development. *American Psychologist, 46,* 333–341. http://dx.doi.org/10.1037/0003-066X.46.4.333

Alarcon, R. D., & Frank, J. B. (Eds.). (2012). *The psychotherapy of hope: The legacy of persuasion and healing.* Baltimore, MD: Johns Hopkins University Press.

Allen, J. G., & Fonagy, P. (Eds.). (2006). *Handbook of mentalization-based treatment.* Chichester, England: Wiley.

Allen, J. G., Fonagy, P., & Bateman, A. W. (2008). *Mentalizing in clinical practice.* Washington, DC: American Psychiatric Publishing.

Allerberger, F. (1997). Julius Wagner-Jauregg (1857–1940). *Journal of Neurology, Neurosurgery, and Psychiatry, 62,* 221–221. http://dx.doi.org/10.1136/jnnp.62.3.221

American Psychological Association. (2012). *Recognition of psychotherapy effectiveness.* Retrieved from http://www.apa.org/about/policy/resolution-psychotherapy.aspx

Anderson, T., Lunnen, K. M., & Ogles, B. M. (2010). Putting models and techniques in context. In B. L. Duncan, S. D. Miller, B. E. Wampold, & M. A. Hubble (Eds.), *The heart and soul of change: Delivering what works in therapy* (2nd ed., pp. 143–166). Washington, DC: American Psychological Association.

Anker, M. G., Duncan, B. L., & Sparks, J. A. (2009). Using client feedback to improve couple therapy outcomes: A randomized clinical trial in a naturalistic setting. *Journal of Consulting and Clinical Psychology, 77,* 693–704. http://dx.doi.org/10.1037/a0016062

Arden, J. B. (2015). *Brain2brain: Enacting client change through the persuasive power of neuroscience.* Hoboken, NJ: Wiley.

Atwood, G., & Stolorow, R. (1984). *Structures of subjectivity: Explorations in psychoanalytic phenomenology.* Hillsdale, NJ: Analytic Press.

Azevedo, F. A. C., Carvalho, L. R. B., Grinberg, L. T., Farfel, J. M., Ferretti, R. E. L., Leite, R. E. P., & Herculano-Houzel, S. (2009). Equal numbers of neuronal and nonneuronal cells make the human brain an isometrically scaled-up primate brain. *The Journal of Comparative Neurology, 513,* 532–541.

Badenoch, B. (2008). *Being a brain-wise therapist: A practical guide to interpersonal neurobiology.* New York, NY: Norton.

Baker, T. B., McFall, R. M., & Shoham, V. (2009). Current status and future prospects of clinical psychology: Toward a scientifically principled approach to mental and behavioral healthcare. *Psychological Science in the Public Interest, 9*(2), 67–103.

Baldwin, S. A., & Imel, Z. (2013). Therapist effects. In M. J. Lambert (Ed.), *Bergin and Garfield's handbook of psychotherapy and behavioral change* (6th ed., pp. 258–297). Hoboken, NJ: Wiley.

Bartholomew K., & Horowitz L. M. (1991). Attachment styles among young adults: A test of a four-category model. *Journal of Personality and Social Psychology, 61,* 226–244.

Bateman, A. W., & Fonagy, P. (Eds.). (2012). *Handbook of mentalizing in mental health practice.* Washington, DC: American Psychiatric Publishing.

Battey, R. (1872). Normal ovariotomy—case. *Atlanta Medical and Surgical Journal, 10,* 321–339.

Battey, R. (1876). Extirpation of the functionally active ovaries for the remedy of otherwise incurable diseases. *Transaction of the American Gynecological Society, 1,* 101–120.

Beckes, L., & Simpson, J. A. (2012). Evolutionary perspectives on caring and prosocial behavior in relationships. In O. Gillath, G. Adams, & A. Kunkel (Eds.), *Relationship science: Integrating evolutionary, neuroscience, and sociocultural approaches* (pp. 27–47). Washington, DC: American Psychological Association.

Benedetti, F. (2008). *Placebo effects: Understanding the mechanisms in health and disease.* New York, NY: Oxford University Press. http://dx.doi.org/10.1093/acprof:oso/9780199559121.001.0001

Benedetti, F. (2011). *The patient's brain: The neuroscience behind the doctor–patient relationship.* New York, NY: Oxford University Press.

Benedetti, F., & Amanzio, M. (1997). The neurobiology of placebo analgesia: From endogenous opioids to cholecystokinin. *Progress in Neurobiology, 52,* 109–125. http://dx.doi.org/10.1016/S0301-0082(97)00006-3

Benedetti, F., Maggi, G., Lopiano, L., Lanotte, M., Rainero, I., Vighetti, S., & Pollo, A. (2003). Open versus hidden medical treatments: The patient's knowledge about a therapy affects the therapy outcome. *Prevention & Treatment, 6,* 23–26. http://dx.doi.org/10.1037/1522-3736.6.1.61a

Benish, S. G., Imel, Z. E., & Wampold, B. E. (2008). The relative efficacy of bona fide psychotherapies for treating post-traumatic stress disorder: A meta-analysis of direct comparisons. *Clinical Psychology Review, 28,* 746–758. http://dx.doi.org/10.1016/j.cpr.2007.10.005

Bergin, A. E., & Lambert, M. J. (1978). The evaluation of outcomes in psychotherapy. In A. E. Bergin & S. L. Garfield (Eds.), *Handbook of psychotherapy and behavior change* (pp. 217–270). New York, NY: Wiley.

Berkman, L. F., & Syme, S. L. (1979). Social networks, host resistance, and mortality: A nine-year follow-up study of Alameda County residents. *American Journal of Epidemiology, 109,* 186–204.

Beutler, L. E., Malik, M., Alimohamed, S., Harwood, T. M., Talebi, H., Noble, S., & Wong, E. (2004). Therapist variables. In M. J. Lambert (Ed.), *Bergin and Garfield's handbook of psychotherapy and behavior change* (5th ed., pp. 227–306). New York, NY: Wiley.

Bike, D. H., Norcross, J. C., & Schatz, D. M. (2009). Processes and outcomes of psychotherapists' personal therapy: Replication and extension 20 years later. *Psychotherapy, 46,* 119–131.

Bohart, A. C., & Greening, T. (2001). Humanistic psychology and positive psychology. *American Psychologist, 56,* 81–82. http://dx.doi.org/10.1037/0003-066X.56.1.81

Bohart, A., & Tallman, K. (1996). The active client: Therapy as self-help. *Journal of Humanistic Psychology, 36,* 7–30. http://dx.doi.org/10.1177/00221678960363002

Bohart, A., & Tallman, K. (1999). *How clients make therapy work: The process of active self-healing.* Washington, DC: American Psychological Association. http://dx.doi.org/10.1037/10323-000

Bohart, A., & Tallman, K. (2010). Clients: The neglected common factor in psychotherapy. In B. Duncan, S. Miller, B. Wampold, & M. Hubble (Eds.), *The heart and soul of change: Delivering what works in therapy* (2nd ed., pp. 83–111). Washington, DC: American Psychological Association. http://dx.doi.org/10.1037/12075-003

Bola, J. R., & Mosher, L. R. (2003). Treatment of acute psychosis without neuroleptics: Two-year outcomes from the Soteria project. *Journal of Nervous and Mental Disease, 191,* 219–229. http://dx.doi.org/10.1097/01.NMD.0000061148.84257.F9

Bowlby, J. (1944). Forty-four juvenile thieves: Their characters and home life. *The International Journal of Psychoanalysis, 25,* 107–127.

Bowlby, J. (1951). *Maternal care and mental health.* Geneva, Switzerland: World Health Organization.

Bowlby, J. (1953). *Child care and the growth of love.* London, England: Penguin Books.

Bowlby, J. (1969). *Attachment and loss: Vol. 1. Attachment.* New York, NY: Basic Books.

Bowlby, J. (1973). *Attachment and loss: Vol. 2. Separation, anxiety, and anger.* New York, NY: Basic Books.

Bowlby, J. (1979). *The making and breaking of affectional bonds.* London, England: Tavistock.

Bowlby, J. (1980). *Attachment and loss: Vol. 3. Loss, sadness, and depression.* New York, NY: Basic Books.

Bowlby, J. (1988). *A secure base: Clinical applications of attachment theory.* London, England: Routledge.

Bozarth, J. D., Zimring, F. M., & Tausch, R. (2001). Client-centered therapy: The evolution of a revolution. In D. J. Cain & J. Seeman (Eds.), *Humanistic psychotherapies: Handbook of research and practice* (pp. 147–188). Washington, DC: American Psychological Association.

Bracken, P., Thomas, P., Timimi, S., Asen, E., Behr, G., Beuster, C., . . . Yeomans, D. (2012). Psychiatry beyond the current paradigm. *The British Journal of Psychiatry, 201,* 430–434. http://dx.doi.org/10.1192/bjp.bp.112.109447

Bradbury, S. (1967). *The evolution of the microscope.* Oxford, England: Pergamon Press.

Braslow, J. T. (1996). In the name of therapeutics: The practice of sterilization in a California State Hospital. *Journal of the History of Medicine and Allied Sciences, 51,* 29–51. http://dx.doi.org/10.1093/jhmas/51.1.29

Breasted, J. H. (1991). *The Edwin Smith surgical papyrus: Published in facsimile and hieroglyphic transliteration with translation and commentary in two volumes* (Vols. 3–4). Chicago, IL: University of Chicago Press.

Breggin, P. (1991). *Toxic psychiatry: Why empathy, therapy and love must replace the drugs, electroshock and biochemical theories of the "new psychiatry."* New York, NY: St. Martin's Press.

Bretherton, I. (1992). The origins of attachment theory: John Bowlby and Mary Ainsworth. *Developmental Psychology, 28,* 759–775. http://dx.doi.org/10.1037/0012-1649.28.5.759

Brisch, K. H. (2011). *Treatment attachment disorders* (2nd ed.). New York, NY: Guilford Press.

Brodsky, A. (2004). *Benjamin Rush: Patriot and physician.* New York, NY: St. Martin's Press.

Brown, E. M. (2000). Why Wagner-Jauregg won the Nobel Prize for discovering malarial therapy for general paresis of the insane. *History of Psychiatry, 11,* 371–382.

Brüne, M., Ribbert, H., & Schiefenhövel, W. (Eds.). (2003). *The social brain: Evolution and pathology.* Hoboken, NJ: Wiley. http://dx.doi.org/10.1002/0470867221

Burns, D. D., & Nolen-Hoeksema, S. (1992). Therapeutic empathy and recovery from depression in cognitive-behavioral therapy: A structural equation model. *Journal of Consulting and Clinical Psychology, 60,* 441–449. http://dx.doi.org/10.1037/0022-006X.60.3.441

Byrne, R. W., & Whiten, A. (1988). *Machiavellian intelligence: Social expertise and the evolution of intellect in monkeys, apes and humans.* Oxford, England: Clarendon Press.

Cain, D. J., & Seeman, J. (Eds.). (2002). *Humanistic psychotherapies: Handbook of research and practice.* Washington, DC: American Psychological Association. http://dx.doi.org/10.1037/10439-000

Cajal, S. R. (1996). *Recollections of my life.* Cambridge, MA: MIT Press.

Carr, L., Iacoboni, M., Dubeau, M. C., Mazziotta, J. C., & Lenzi, G. L. (2003). Neural mechanisms of empathy in humans: A relay from neural systems for imitation to limbic areas. *Proceedings of the National Academy of Sciences, USA, 100,* 5497–5502. http://dx.doi.org/10.1073/pnas.0935845100

Cassidy, J. (1999). The nature of a child's ties. In J. Cassidy & P. R. Shaver (Eds.), *Handbook of attachment: Theory, research and clinical applications* (pp. 3–20). New York, NY: Guilford Press.

Cassidy, J., & Shaver, P. R. (Eds.). (2010). *Handbook of attachment: Theory, research, and clinical applications* (2nd ed.). New York, NY: Guilford Press.

Charland, L. C. (2007). Benevolent theory: Moral treatment at the York Retreat. *History of Psychiatry, 18*, 61–80. http://dx.doi.org/10.1177/0957154X07070320

Cherry, C. L. (1989). *A quiet haven: Quakers, moral treatment, and asylum reform.* London, England: Associated University Press.

Chodoff, P. (1982). Hysteria and women. *The American Journal of Psychiatry, 139*, 545–551.

Ciompi, L., & Hoffman, H. (2004). Soteria Berne: An innovative milieu therapeutic approach to acute schizophrenia based on the concept of affect-logic. *World Psychiatry, 3*, 140–146.

Cohen, S. (2001). Social relationships and health: Berkman & Syme (1979). *Advances in Mind-Body Medicine, 17*, 5–7. http://dx.doi.org/10.1054/ambm.2000.0244

Cohen, S. (2004). Social relationships and health. *American Psychologist, 59*, 676–684.

Cohen, S., Doyle, W. J., Skoner, D. P., Rabin, B. S., & Gwaltney, J. M., Jr. (1997). Social ties and susceptibility to the common cold. *JAMA, 277*, 1940–1944. http://dx.doi.org/10.1001/jama.1997.03540480040036

Conolly, J. (1847). *The construction and government of lunatic asylums and hospitals for the insane.* London, England: John Churchill.

Costa, A. L., & O'Leary, P. W. (Eds.). (2013). *The power of the social brain: Teaching, learning, and interdependent thinking.* New York, NY: Teachers College Press.

Costello, P. C. (2013). *Attachment-based psychotherapy.* Washington, DC: American Psychological Association.

Coyle, J. T. (2000). Psychotropic drug use in very young children. *JAMA, 283*, 1059–1060. http://dx.doi.org/10.1001/jama.283.8.1059

Cozolino, L. (2010). *The neuroscience of psychotherapy: Healing the social brain.* New York, NY: Norton.

Cozolino, L. (2014). *The neuroscience of human relationships: Attachment and the developing social brain* (2nd ed.). New York, NY: Norton.

Crits-Christoph, P., Baranackie, K., Kurcias, J. S., Beck, A. T., Carroll, K., Perry, K., . . . Zitrin, C. (1991). Meta-analysis of therapist effects in psychotherapy outcome studies. *Psychotherapy Research, 1*, 81–91. http://dx.doi.org/10.1080/10503309112331335511

Dale, H. H. (1906). On some physiological actions of ergot. *The Journal of Physiology, 34*, 163–164.

Dally, A. (1996). *Fantasy surgery, 1880–1930.* Atlanta, GA: Editions Rodopi.

Decety, J., & Ickes, W. (Eds.). (2011). *The social neuroscience of empathy.* Cambridge, MA: MIT Press.

Digby, A. (1984). The changing profile of a nineteenth-century asylum: The York Retreat. *Psychological Medicine, 14*, 739–748. http://dx.doi.org/10.1017/S003329170001970X

Digby, A. (1985). *Madness, morality and medicine: A study of the York Retreat, 1796–1914*. Cambridge, MA: Cambridge University Press.

di Pellegrino, G., Fadiga, L., Fogassi, L., Gallese, V., & Rizzolatti, G. (1992). Understanding motor events: A neurophysiological study. *Experimental Brain Research, 91*, 176–180. http://dx.doi.org/10.1007/BF00230027

Domes, G., Heinrichs, M., Michel, A., Berger, C., & Herpertz, S. C. (2007). Oxytocin improves "mind-reading" in humans. *Biological Psychiatry, 61*, 731–733. http://dx.doi.org/10.1016/j.biopsych.2006.07.015

Dowbiggen, I. (2011). *The quest for mental health: A tale of science, medicine, scandal, sorrow, and mass society*. Cambridge, England: Cambridge University Press.

Dunbar, R. I. M. (1988). *Primate social systems*. New Haven, CT: Yale University Press. http://dx.doi.org/10.1007/978-1-4684-6694-2

Dunbar, R. I. M. (1998). The social brain hypothesis. *Evolutionary Anthropology, 6*, 178–190. http://dx.doi.org/10.1002/(SICI)1520-6505(1998)6:5<178::AID-EVAN5>3.0.CO;2-8

Dunbar, R. I. M. (2009). The social brain hypothesis and its implications for social evolution. *Annals of Human Biology, 36*, 562–572. http://dx.doi.org/10.1080/03014460902960289

Dunbar, R. I. M., Gamble, C., & Gowlett, J. (Eds.). (2010). *Social brain, distributed mind*. London, England: British Academy. http://dx.doi.org/10.5871/bacad/9780197264522.001.0001

Dunbar, R. I. M., & Shultz, S. (2007). Evolution in the social brain. *Science, 317*, 1344–1347. http://dx.doi.org/10.1126/science.1145463

Duncan, B. L. (2010a). A conversation with Saul Rosenzweig. In B. L. Duncan, S. D. Miller, B. E. Wampold, & M. A. Hubble (Eds.), *The heart and soul of change: Delivering what works in therapy* (2nd ed., pp. 13–20). Washington, DC: American Psychological Association. http://dx.doi.org/10.1037/12075-000

Duncan, B. L. (2010b). *On becoming a better therapist*. Washington, DC: American Psychological Association. http://dx.doi.org/10.1037/12080-000

Duncan, B. L. (2014). *On becoming a better therapist: Evidence-based practice one client at a time* (2nd ed.). Washington, DC: American Psychological Association. http://dx.doi.org/10.1037/14392-000

Duncan, B. L., Hubble, M. A., & Miller, S. (1997). *Psychotherapy with "impossible" cases: Efficient treatment of therapy veterans*. New York, NY: Norton.

Duncan, B. L., Miller, S. D., Wampold, B. E., & Hubble, M. A. (Eds.). (2010). *The heart and soul of change: Delivering what works in therapy* (2nd ed.). Washington, DC: American Psychological Association. http://dx.doi.org/10.1037/12075-000

Duncan, B. L., Miller, S. D., & Sparks, J. A. (2004). *The heroic client: A revolutionary way to improve effectiveness through client-centered, outcome-informed therapy* (Rev. ed.). San Francisco, CA: Jossey-Bass.

Duncan, B. L., & Reese, R. J. (2012). Empirically supported treatments, evidence based treatments, and evidence based practice. In G. Stricker and T. Widiger (Eds.), *Handbook of psychology: Clinical psychology* (2nd ed., pp. 977–1023). Hoboken. NJ: Wiley.

Duncan, B., & Moynihan, D. (1994). Applying outcome research: Intentional utilization of the client's frame of reference. *Psychotherapy: Theory, Research, Practice, Training, 31,* 294–301. http://dx.doi.org/10.1037/h0090215

Duncan, B., Solovey, A., & Rusk, G. (1992). *Changing the rules: A client-directed approach.* New York, NY: Guilford Press.

Earle, P. (1887). *The curability of insanity.* Philadelphia, PA: Lippincott. http://dx.doi.org/10.1037/10779-000

Eisenberger, N. I., & Lieberman, M. D. (2004). Why rejection hurts: A common neural alarm system for physical and social pain. *Trends in Cognitive Sciences, 8,* 294–300. http://dx.doi.org/10.1016/j.tics.2004.05.010

Eliade, M. (1964). *Shamanism.* Princeton, NJ: Princeton University Press.

Elkins, D. N. (2007). Empirically supported treatments: The deconstruction of a myth. *Journal of Humanistic Psychology, 47,* 474–500.

Elkins, D. N. (2009a). The medical model in psychotherapy: Its limitation and failures. *Journal of Humanistic Psychology, 49,* 66–84. http://dx.doi.org/10.1177/0022167807307901

Elkins, D. N. (2009b). *Humanistic psychology: A clinical manifesto: A critique of clinical psychology and the need for progressive alternatives.* Colorado Springs, CO: University of the Rockies Press.

Elkins, D. N. (2012a). Toward a common focus in psychotherapy research. *Psychotherapy: Theory, Research, Practice, Training, 49,* 450–454. http://dx.doi.org/10.1037/a0027797

Elkins, D. N. (2012b). The humanistic and behavioral traditions: Areas of agreement and disagreement. *Psychotherapy: Theory, Research, Practice, Training, 49,* 465–468.

Ertel, K. A., Glymour, M. M., & Berkman, L. F. (2009). Social networks and health: A life course perspective integrating observational and experimental evidence. *Journal of Social and Personal Relationships, 26,* 73–92.

Etkin, A., Phil, M., Pittenger, C., Polan, J., & Kandel, E. R. (2005). Toward a neurobiology of psychotherapy: Basic science and clinical applications. *The Journal of Neuropsychiatry and Clinical Neurosciences, 17,* 145–158.

Everson-Rose, S. A., & Lewis, T. T. (2005). Psychosocial factors and cardiovascular disease. *Annual Review of Public Health, 26,* 469–500.

Field, T. (1978). Interaction behaviours of primary versus secondary caretaker fathers. *Developmental Psychology, 14,* 183–184. http://dx.doi.org/10.1037/0012-1649.14.2.183.

Finger, S. (1994). *Origins of neuroscience: A history of explorations into brain functions.* New York, NY: Oxford University Press.

Finger, S. (2000). *Minds behind the brain: A history of the pioneers and their discoveries.* New York, NY: Oxford University Press.

Fink, M. (1979). *Convulsive therapy: Theory and practice.* New York, NY: Raven.

Fonagy, P., Bateman, A. W., & Luyten, P. (2012). Introduction and overview. In A. W. Bateman & P. Fonagy (Eds.). *Handbook of mentalizing in mental health practice.* (pp. 3–42). Washington, DC: American Psychiatric Publishing.

Foucault, M. (1965). *Madness and civilization: A history of insanity in the age of reason.* Cambridge, England: Tavistock Press.

Frank, J. D. (1961). *Persuasion and healing: A comparative study of psychotherapy.* Baltimore, MD: Johns Hopkins University Press.

Frank, J. D. (1973). *Persuasion and healing: A comparative study of psychotherapy* (2nd ed.). Baltimore, MD: Johns Hopkins University Press.

Frank, J. D., & Frank, J. B. (1991). *Persuasion and healing: A comparative study of psychotherapy* (3rd ed.). Baltimore, MD: Johns Hopkins University Press.

Fromm-Reichmann, F. (1950). *Principles of intensive psychotherapy.* Chicago, IL: University of Chicago Press

Fu, C. H. Y., Williams, S. C. R., Cleare, A. J., Scott, J., Mitterschiffthaler, M. T., Walsh, N. D., . . . Murray, R. M. (2008). Neural responses to sad facial expressions in major depression following cognitive behavioral therapy. *Biological Psychiatry, 64,* 505–512. http://dx.doi.org/10.1016/j.biopsych.2008.04.033

Garfield, S. L. (1992). Eclectic psychotherapy: A common factors approach. In J. C. Norcross & M. R. Goldfried (Eds.), *Handbook of psychotherapy integration* (pp. 169–201). New York, NY: Basic Books.

Gerard, D. L. (1998). Chiarugi and Pinel considered: Soul's brain/person's mind. *Journal of the History of the Behavioral Sciences, 33,* 381–403. http://dx.doi.org/10.1002/(SICI)1520-6696(199723)33:4<381::AID-JHBS3>3.0.CO;2-S

Glover, M. R. (1984). *The retreat York: Early Quaker experiment in the treatment of mental illness.* York, England: William Sessions.

Goetz, J. L., Keltner, D., & Simon-Thomas, E. (2010). Compassion: An evolutionary analysis and empirical review. *Psychological Bulletin, 136,* 351–374. http://dx.doi.org/10.1037/a0018807

Goldapple, K., Segal, Z., Garson, C., Lau, M., Bieling, P., Kennedy, S., & Mayberg, H. (2004). Modulation of cortical-limbic pathways in major depression: Treatment-specific effects of cognitive behavior therapy. *Archives of General Psychiatry, 61,* 34–41. http://dx.doi.org/10.1001/archpsyc.61.1.34

Goldsmith, L. P., Lewis, S. W., Dunn, G., & Bentall, R. P. (2015). Psychological treatments for early psychosis can be beneficial or harmful, depending on the therapeutic alliance: An instrumental variable analysis. *Psychological Medicine, 4,* 1–9.

Goodheart, L. (2003). *Mad Yankees: The Hartford Retreat for the insane and nineteenth-century psychiatry.* Amherst, MA: University of Massachusetts Press.

Gordon, M. (2009). *Roots of empathy: Changing the world child by child.* New York, NY: Thomas Allen.

Grange, K. M. (1961). Pinel and eighteenth century psychiatry. *Bulletin for the History of Medicine, 35,* 442–453.

Grawe, K. (2007). *Neuropsychotherapy: How the neurosciences inform effective psychotherapy.* New York, NY: Taylor & Francis.

Graziano, M. S. A. (2013). *Consciousness and the social brain.* New York, NY: Oxford University Press.

Grob, G. N. (1973). *Mental institutions in America: Social policy to 1875.* New York, NY: Free Press.

Grossman, K. E., Grossman, K., & Waters, E. (2005). *Attachment from infancy to adulthood.* New York, NY: Guilford Press.

Haarer, J. (1934). *The German mother and her first child.* Munich, Germany: Lehmanns.

Harlow, H. F. (1958). The nature of love. *American Psychologist, 13,* 673–685. http://dx.doi.org/10.1037/h0047884

Harlow, H. F. (1962). Development of affection in privates. In E. L. Bliss (Ed.), *Roots of behavior* (pp. 157–166). New York, NY: Harper & Row.

Harlow, H. F. (1964). Early social deprivation and later behavior in the monkey. In A. Abrams, H. H. Gurner, & J. E. P. Tomal (Eds.), *Unfinished tasks in the behavioral sciences* (pp. 154–173). Baltimore, MD: Williams & Wilkins.

Hart, S. (2010). *The impact of attachment.* New York, NY: Norton.

Hazan, C., & Shaver, P. (1987). Romantic love conceptualized as an attachment process. *Journal of Personality and Social Psychology, 52,* 511–524. http://dx.doi.org/10.1037/0022-3514.52.3.511

Hazan, C., & Shaver, P. R. (1990). Love and work: An attachment theoretical perspective. *Journal of Personality and Social Psychology, 59,* 270–280. http://dx.doi.org/10.1037/0022-3514.59.2.270

Hazan, C., & Shaver, P. R. (1994). Attachment as an organizational framework for research on close relationships. *Psychological Inquiry, 5,* 1–22. http://dx.doi.org/10.1207/s15327965pli0501_1

Herculano-Houzel, S. (2009). The human brain in numbers: A linearly scaled-up primate brain. *Frontiers in Human Neuroscience, 3*(article 31). http://dx.doi.org/10.3389/neuro.09.031.2009

Hollon, S. D., Stewart, M. O., & Strunk, D. (2006). Enduring effects for cognitive behavior therapy in the treatment of depression and anxiety. *Annual Review of Psychology, 57,* 285–315. http://dx.doi.org/10.1146/annurev.psych.57.102904.190044

Holt-Lunstad, J., Smith, T. B., & Layton, J. B. (2010). Social relationships and mortality risk: A meta-analytic review. *PLoS Medicine, 7*(7), e1000316. http://dx.doi.org/10.1371/journal.pmed.1000316

Hood, B. (2012). *The self illusion: How the social brain creates identity.* New York, NY: Oxford University Press.

Horvath, A., Del Re, A. C., Flückiger, C., & Symonds, D. (2011). Alliance in individual psychotherapy. *Psychotherapy: Theory, Research, Practice, Training, 48,* 9–16.

House, J. S., Landis, K. R., & Umberson, D. (1999). *Social relationships and health.* New York, NY: New Press.

Hubble, M. A., Duncan, B. L., & Miller, S. D. (Eds.). (1999). *The heart and soul of change: What works in therapy.* Washington, DC: American Psychological Association. http://dx.doi.org/10.1037/11132-000

Hubble, M. A., Duncan, B. L., Miller, S. D., & Wampold, B. E. (2010). Introduction. In B. L. Duncan, S. D. Miller, B. E. Wampold, & M. A. Hubble (Eds.), *The heart and soul of change: Delivering what works in therapy* (2nd ed., pp. 23–46). Washington, DC: American Psychological Association.

Hunter, R., & MacAlpine, I. (1982). *Three hundred years of psychiatry, 1535–1860.* Hartsdale, NY: Carlisle.

Hutton, R. (1999). *The triumph of the moon: A history of modern pagan witchcraft.* Oxford, England: Oxford University Press. http://dx.doi.org/10.1093/acprof:oso/9780198207443.001.0001

Iacoboni, M. (2009). *Mirroring people: The science of empathy and how we connect with others.* New York, NY: Farrar, Straus, & Giroux.

Imel, Z. E., Malterer, M. B., McKay, K. M., & Wampold, B. E. (2008). A meta-analysis of psychotherapy and medication in unipolar depression and dysthymia. *Journal of Affective Disorders, 110,* 197–206. http://dx.doi.org/10.1016/j.jad.2008.03.018

Imel, Z. E., Wampold, B. E., Miller, S. D., & Fleming, R. R. (2008). Distinctions without a difference: Direct comparisons of psychotherapies for alcohol use disorders. *Psychology of Addictive Behaviors, 22,* 533–543. http://dx.doi.org/10.1037/a0013171

Ipser, J. C., Singh, L., & Stein, D. J. (2013). Meta-analysis of functional brain imaging in specific phobia. *Psychiatry and Clinical Neurosciences, 67,* 311–322. http://dx.doi.org/10.1111/pcn.12055

Isaacs, S. (1948). The nature and function of phantasy. *International Journal of Psychoanalysis, 29,* 73–98.

Ivey, A. E., & Zalaquett, C. P. (2011). Neuroscience and counseling: Central issue for social justice leaders. *Journal of Social Action in Counseling and Psychology, 3,* 103–116.

Jimenez, M. A. (1987). *Changing faces of madness: Early American attitudes and treatment of the insane.* Hanover, NH: University Press of New England.

Jolly, A. (1966). Lemur social behavior and primate intelligence. *Science, 153,* 501–506. http://dx.doi.org/10.1126/science.153.3735.501

Jones, K. (1996). Foreword. In S. Tuke (author), *Description of the retreat: An institution near York, for insane persons of the Society of Friends* (1813; pp. vii–xv). London, England: Process Press.

Kagan, J. (2000). *Three seductive ideas.* Cambridge, MA: Harvard University Press.

Kandel, E. R. (1998). A new intellectual framework for psychiatry. *The American Journal of Psychiatry, 155,* 457–469. http://dx.doi.org/10.1176/ajp.155.4.457

Kandel, E. R., Schwartz, J. H., & Jessell, T. M. (2000). *Principles of neural science* (4th ed.). New York, NY: McGraw-Hill.

Karen, R. (1998). *Becoming attached: First relationships and how they shape our capacity to love.* New York, NY: Oxford University Press.

Katz, B. (1966). *Nerve, muscle, and synapse.* New York, NY: McGraw-Hill.

Katz, B. (1969). *The release of neural transmitter substances* (The Sherrington Lectures X). Springfield, IL: Charles C Thomas.

Kelly, G. A. (1955). *The psychology of personal constructs* (Vols. 1 and 2). New York, NY: Norton.

Kelly, G. A. (1963). *A theory of personality: The psychology of personal constructs.* New York, NY: Norton.

Kendell, R. E. (2001). The distinction between mental and physical illness. *The British Journal of Psychiatry, 178,* 490–493. http://dx.doi.org/10.1192/bjp.178.6.490

Keysers, C. (2011). *The empathic brain: How the discovery of mirror neurons changes our understanding of human nature* [Kindle E-Book]. Retrieved from http://www.amazon.com

Kim, D.-M., Wampold, B. E., & Bolt, D. M. (2006). Therapist effects in psychotherapy: A random-effects modeling of the National Institute of Mental Health Treatment of Depression Collaborative Research Program data. *Psychotherapy Research, 16,* 161–172. http://dx.doi.org/10.1080/10503300500264911

Kirschenbaum, H. (2009). *The life and work of Carl Rogers.* Alexandria, VA: American Counseling Association.

Kirschenbaum, H., & Jourdan, A. (2005). The current status of Carl Rogers and the person-centered approach. *Psychotherapy: Theory, Research, Practice, Training, 42,* 37–51. http://dx.doi.org/10.1037/0033-3204.42.1.37

Klein, M. (1932). *The psycho-analysis of children.* London, England: Hogarth Press.

Klein, M. (1975). *The collected writings of Melanie Klein* (Vols. 1–4). London, England: Hogarth Press.

Kosfeld, M., Heinrichs, M., Zak, P. J., Fischbacher, U., & Fehr, E. (2005, June). Oxytocin increases trust in humans. *Nature, 435,* 673–676. http://dx.doi.org/10.1038/nature03701

Kraepelin, E. (1962). *One hundred years of psychiatry.* New York, NY: Philosophical Library.

Kumari, V., Fannon, D., Peters, E. R., Ffytche, D. H., Sumich, A. L., Premkumar, P., . . . Kuipers, E. (2011). Neural changes following cognitive behaviour therapy for psychosis: A longitudinal study. *Brain: A Journal of Neurology, 134,* 2396–2407. http://dx.doi.org/10.1093/brain/awr154

Lafferty, P., Beutler, L. E., & Crago, M. (1989). Differences between more and less effective psychotherapists: A study of select therapist variables. *Journal of Consulting and Clinical Psychology, 57,* 76–80. http://dx.doi.org/10.1037/0022-006X.57.1.76

Lambert, M. J. (1986). Implications of psychotherapy outcome research for eclectic psychotherapy. In J. C. Norcross (Ed.), *Handbook of eclectic psychotherapy* (pp. 436–462). New York, NY: Brunner/Mazel.

Lambert, M. J. (1992). Psychotherapy outcome research: Implications for integrative and eclectic therapists. In J. C. Norcross & M. R. Goldfried (Eds.) *Handbook of psychotherapy integration* (pp. 94–129). New York, NY: Basic Books.

Lambert, M. J. (Ed.). (2004). *Bergin and Garfield's handbook of psychotherapy and behavior* (5th ed.). Hoboken, NJ: Wiley.

Lambert, M. J. (2010a). *Prevention of treatment failure: The use of measuring, monitoring, and feedback in clinical practice.* Washington, DC: American Psychological Association. http://dx.doi.org/10.1037/12141-000

Lambert, M. J. (2010b). Yes, it's time for clinicians to routinely monitor treatment outcome. In B. L. Duncan, S. D. Miller, B. E. Wampold, & M. A. Hubble (Eds.), *The heart and soul of change: Delivering what works in therapy* (2nd ed., pp. 239–266). Washington, DC: American Psychological Association. http://dx.doi.org/10.1037/12075-008

Lambert, M. J. (Ed.). (2013). *Bergin and Garfield's handbook of psychotherapy and behavior* (6th ed.). Hoboken, NJ: Wiley.

Lambert, M. J., & Barley, D. E. (2002). Research summary on the therapeutic relationship and psychotherapy outcome. In J. C. Norcross & M. R. Goldfried (Eds.), *Psychotherapy relationships that work* (pp. 17–32). Oxford, England: Oxford University Press.

Lambert, M. J., & Bergin, A. E. (1994). The effectiveness of psychotherapy. In A. E. Bergin & S. L. Garfield (Eds.), *Handbook of psychotherapy and behavior change* (4th ed., pp. 143–189). New York, NY: Wiley.

Lambert, M. J., & Ogle, B. M. (2004). The efficacy and effectiveness of psychotherapy. In M. J. Lambert (Ed.), *Handbook of psychotherapy and behavior change* (5th ed., pp. 139–193). New York, NY: Wiley.

Lambert, M. J., & Shimokawa, K. (2011). Collecting client feedback. *Psychotherapy: Theory, Research, Practice, Training, 48,* 72–79. http://dx.doi.org/10.1037/a0022238

Landman, J. T., & Dawes, R. M. (1982). Psychotherapy outcome: Smith and Glass' conclusions stand up under scrutiny. *American Psychologist, 37,* 504–516. http://dx.doi.org/10.1037/0003-066X.37.5.504

Legerstee, M., Haley, D. W., & Bornstein, M. H. (Eds.). (2013). *The infant mind: Origins of the social brain.* New York, NY: Guilford Press.

Leiknes, K. A., Jarosh-von Schweder, L., & Høie, B. (2012). Contemporary use and practice of electroconvulsive therapy worldwide. *Brain and Behavior, 2,* 283–344. http://dx.doi.org/10.1002/brb3.37

Levack, B. P. (2006). *The witch-hunt in early modern Europe* (3rd ed.). New York, NY: Routledge.

Lipsey, M. W., & Wilson, D. B. (1993). The efficacy of psychological, educational, and behavioral treatment. Confirmation from meta-analysis. *American Psychologist, 48,* 1181–1209. http://dx.doi.org/10.1037/0003-066X.48.12.1181

Lordkipanidze, D., Vekua, A., Ferring, R., Rightmire, G. P., Agusti, J., Kiladze, G., . . . Zollikofer, C. P. (2005). Anthropology: The earliest toothless hominin skull. *Nature, 434,* 717–718. http://dx.doi.org/10.1038/434717b

Lorenz, K. (1970). *Studies in animal and human behavior* (Vol. 1). Cambridge, MA: Harvard University Press.

Lorenz, K. (1971). *Studies in animal and human behavior* (Vol. 2). Cambridge, MA: Harvard University Press.

Lorenz, K. (2007). *King Solomon's ring* (3rd ed.). London, England: Routledge.

Luborsky, L., Singer, B., & Luborsky, L. (1975). Comparative studies of psychotherapies: Is it true that "everyone has won and all must have prizes"? *Archives of General Psychiatry, 32,* 995–1008. http://dx.doi.org/10.1001/archpsyc.1975.01760260059004

Mackay, C. S. (Trans.). (2009). *The hammer of witches: A complete translation of the malleus maleficarum.* New York, NY: Cambridge University Press.

Mackay, R. P. (1965). Ladislas Joseph Meduna 1896–1964. *Recent Advances in Biological Psychiatry, 8,* 357–358.

Maier, T. (2003). *Dr. Spock: An American life.* New York, NY: Basic Books.

Martin, S. D., Martin, E., Rai, S. S., Richardson, M. A., & Royall, R. (2001). Brain blood flow changes in depressed patients treated with interpersonal psychotherapy or venlafaxine hydrochloride: Preliminary findings. *Archives of General Psychiatry, 58,* 641–648. http://dx.doi.org/10.1001/archpsyc.58.7.641

Mazzarello, P., Badiani, A., & Buchtel, H. A. (2010). *Golgi: A biography of the founder of modern neuroscience.* Oxford, England: Oxford University Press.

McGovern, C. M. (1985). *The masters of madness: Social origins to the American psychiatric profession.* New York, NY: Hanover Press.

Mechakra-Tahiri, S., Zunzunegui, M. V., Preville, M., & Dube, M. (2009). Social relationships and depression among people 65 years and over living in rural and urban areas of Quebec. *International Journal of Geriatric Psychiatry, 24*, 1226–1236.

Messer, S. B., & Wampold, B. E. (2002). Let's face the facts: Common factors are more potent than specific therapy ingredients. *Clinical Psychology: Science and Practice, 9*, 21–25. http://dx.doi.org/10.1093/clipsy.9.1.21

Miller, S., Wampold, B., & Varhely, K. (2008). Direct comparisons of treatment modalities for youth disorders: A meta-analysis. *Psychotherapy Research, 18*, 5–14. http://dx.doi.org/10.1080/10503300701472131

Moniz, E. (1956). How I succeeded in performing the prefrontal leukotomy. In A. M. Sackler, M. D. Sackler, R. R. Sackler, & F. Marti-Ibanez (Eds.), *The great physiodynamic therapies in psychiatry: An historical reappraisal* (pp. 131–137). New York, NY: Hoeber.

Mooney, C. G. (2010). *Introduction to attachment: Bowlby, Ainsworth, Gerber, Brazelton, Kennell, and Klaus.* St. Paul, MN: Redleaf.

Mora, G. (1959). Vincenzo Chiarugi (1759–1820) and his psychiatric reform in Florence in the late 18th century (on the occasion of the bi-centenary of his birth). *Journal of the History of Medicine and Allied Sciences, 14*, 424–433.

Mosher, L. R. (1972). Research design to evaluate psychosocial treatments of schizophrenia. In D. Rubenstein & Y. O. Alanen (Eds.), *Psychotherapy of schizophrenia* (pp. 251–260). Amsterdam, The Netherlands: Excerpta Medica Foundation. http://dx.doi.org/10.1176/ps.23.8.229

Mosher, L. R. (1999). Soteria and other alternatives to acute psychiatric hospitalization: A personal and professional review. *Journal of Nervous and Mental Disease, 187*, 142–149. http://dx.doi.org/10.1097/00005053-199903000-00003

Mosher, L. R., & Menn, A. Z. (1977). Soteria House: One-year outcome data [proceedings]. *Psychopharmacology Bulletin, 13*(2), 46–48.

Mosher, L. R., & Menn, A. Z. (1978). Community residential treatment for schizophrenia: Two-year follow-up. *Hospital & Community Psychiatry, 29*, 715–723.

Nagasawa, M., Kikusui, T., Onaka, T., & Ohta, M. (2009). Dog's gaze at its owner increases owner's urinary oxytocin during social interaction. *Hormones and Behavior, 55*, 434–441. http://dx.doi.org/10.1016/j.yhbeh.2008.12.002

Neumann, I. D. (2008). Brain oxytocin: A key regulator of emotional and social behaviours in both females and males. *Journal of Neuroendocrinology, 20*, 858–865. http://dx.doi.org/10.1111/j.1365-2826.2008.01726.x

Norcross, J. C. (2001). Purposes, processes, and products of the task force on empirically supported therapy relationships. *Psychotherapy: Theory, Research, Practice, Training, 38*, 345–356. http://dx.doi.org/10.1037/0033-3204.38.4.345

Norcross, J. C. (Ed.). (2002). *Psychotherapy relationships that work.* Oxford, England: Oxford University Press.

Norcross, J. C. (2010). The therapeutic relationship. In B. L. Duncan, S. D. Miller, B. E. Wampold, & M. A. Hubble (Eds.), *The heart and soul of change: Delivering what works in therapy* (2nd ed., pp. 113–141). Washington, DC: American Psychological Association.

Norcross, J. C., Dryden, W., & DeMichele, J. T. (1992). British clinical psychologists and personal therapy: III. What's good for the goose? *Clinical Psychology Forum, 44,* 29–33.

Nunn, J. F. (1996). *Ancient Egyptian medicine.* Norman: University of Oklahoma Press.

Orlinsky, D., Grave, K., & Parks, B. K. (1994). Process and outcome in psychotherapy: Noch einmal. In A. E. Bergin & S. L. Garfield (Eds.), *Handbook of psychotherapy and behavior change* (pp. 257–310). New York, NY: Wiley.

Orlinsky, D., Ronnestad, M. H., & Willutzki, U. (2004). Fifty years of process-outcome research: Continuity and change. In M. J. Lambert (Ed.), *Bergin and Garfield's handbook of psychotherapy and behavior change* (5th ed., pp. 307–390). New York, NY: Wiley.

Ott, I., & Scott, J. C. (1910). The action of infundibulum upon mammary secretion. *Proceedings of the Royal Society for Experimental Biology, 8,* 48–49. http://dx.doi.org/10.3181/00379727-8-27

Parry-Jones, W. L. (1972). *The trade in lunacy: A study of private madhouses in England in the eighteenth and nineteenth centuries.* London, England: Routledge.

Phan, K. L., Wager, T., Taylor, S. F., & Liberzon, I. (2002). Functional neuroanatomy of emotion: A meta-analysis of emotion activation studies in PET and fMRI. *NeuroImage, 16,* 331–348. http://dx.doi.org/10.1006/nimg.2002.1087

Pietromonaco, P. R., & Barrett, L. F. (1997). Working models of attachment and daily social interactions. *Journal of Personality and Social Psychology, 73,* 1409–1423. http://dx.doi.org/10.1037/0022-3514.73.6.1409

Pinel, P. (1799). Recherches et observations sur le traitement moral des alineens [Research and observations on the moral treatment of lunatics]. *Memoires de la Societe medicale d'emulation de Paris, 7,* 215–255.

Pinel, P. (1801). *Traité medico-philosophique sur l'aliénation mentale ou la Manie* [Medico-philosophical treatise on lunacy or mania]. Paris, France: Caille and Ravier.

Pinel, P. (1962). *A treatise on insanity.* New York, NY: Hafner. (Original work published 1806)

Pinel, P. (2008). *Medico-philosophical treatise on mental alienation: Entirely reworked and extensively expanded (1809)* (2nd ed.). Chichester, England:

Wiley. (Original work published 1809) http://dx.doi.org/10.1002/9780470712238

Pope, K. S., & Tabachnick, B. G. (1994). Therapists as patients: A national survey of psychologists' experiences, problems, and beliefs. *Professional Psychology: Research and Practice, 25,* 247–258.

Porter, R. (1998). *The greatest benefit to mankind: A medical history of humanity.* New York, NY: Norton.

Porter, R. (2002). *Madness: A brief history.* Oxford, England: Oxford University Press.

Porter, R. (2004). *Madmen: A social history of madhouses, mad doctors & lunatics.* Stroud, England: Tempus.

Prasko, J., Horácek, J., Záleský, R., Kopecek, M., Novák, T., Pasková, B., . . . Höschl, C. (2004). The change of regional brain metabolism (18FDG PET) in panic disorder during the treatment with cognitive behavioral therapy or antidepressants. *Neuroendocrinology Letters, 25,* 340–348.

Rachman, S. J., & Wilson, G. T. (1980). *The effects of psychological therapy* (2nd ed.). New York, NY: Pergamon Press.

Rholes, W. S., & Simpson, J. A. (2004). Attachment theory: Basic concepts and contemporary questions. In W. S. Rholes & J. A. Simpson (Eds.), *Adult attachment: Theory, research, and clinical implications* (pp. 3–14). New York, NY: Guilford Press.

Rholes, W. S., & Simpson, J. A. (Eds.). (2004). *Adult attachment: Theory, research, and clinical implications* (pp. 3–14). New York, NY: Guilford Press.

Richerson, P. J., & Boyd, R. (1998). The evolution of human ultra-sociality. In I. Eibl-Eibisfeldt & F. Salter (Eds.), *Ideology, warfare, and indoctrinability* (pp. 71–95). New York, NY: Berghahn Books.

Richerson, P. J., & Boyd, R. (2005). *Not by genes alone: How culture transformed human evolution.* Chicago, IL: University of Chicago Press.

Robinson, L. A., Berman, J. S., & Neimeyer, R. A. (1990). Psychotherapy for the treatment of depression: A comprehensive review of controlled outcome research. *Psychological Bulletin, 108,* 30–49. http://dx.doi.org/10.1037/0033-2909.108.1.30

Rogers, C. R. (1951). *Client-centered therapy.* Boston, MA: Houghton Mifflin.

Rogers, C. R. (1957). The necessary and sufficient conditions of therapeutic personality change. *Journal of Consulting Psychology, 21,* 95–103. http://dx.doi.org/10.1037/h0045357

Rogers, C. R. (1959). A theory of therapy, personality and interpersonal relationships as developed in the client-centered framework. In S. Koch (Ed.), *Psychology: A study of a science* (Vol. 3; pp. 184–246). New York, NY: McGraw Hill.

Rogers, C. R. (1977). *Carl Rogers on personal power.* New York, NY: Delacorte Press.

Rogers, C. R., & Dymond, R. F. (Eds.). (1954). *Psychotherapy and personality change: Co-ordinated research studies in the client-centered approach.* Chicago, IL: University of Chicago Press.

Rogers, N. (2008). *Carl Rogers.* Retrieved from http://www.nrogers.com/carlrogers.html

Roper, L. (1994). *Oedipus and the devil: Witchcraft, sexuality and religion in early modern Europe.* New York, NY: Routledge. http://dx.doi.org/10.4324/9780203426296

Rosenzweig, S. (1936). Some implicit common factors in diverse methods of psychotherapy. *American Journal of Orthopsychiatry, 6,* 412–415. http://dx.doi.org/10.1111/j.1939-0025.1936.tb05248.x

Rush, B. (1962). *Medical inquiries and observations upon the diseases of the mind.* Philadelphia, PA: Kimber and Richardson. (Original work published 1812)

Rutter, M. (1972). *Maternal deprivation reassessed.* Harmondsworth, England: Penguin.

Rutter, M. (1981). *Maternal deprivation reassessed* (2nd ed.). Harmondsworth, England: Penguin.

Sable, P. (2001). *Attachment and adult psychotherapy.* New York, NY: Jason Aronson.

Sakel, M. (1994). The methodical use of hypoglicemia (sic) in the treatment of psychoses. *The American Journal of Psychiatry, 151,* 240–247.

Satel, S., & Lilienfeld, S. O. (2013). *Brainwashed: The seductive appeal of mindless neuroscience.* New York, NY: Basic Books.

Schafer, E. A., & MacKenzie, K. (1911). The action of animal abstracts on milk secretion. *Proceedings of the Royal Society of London. Series B, Containing Papers of a Biological Character, 84*(568), 16–22.

Schaffer, H. R. (1996). *Social development: An introduction.* Oxford, England: Blackwell.

Schienle, A., Schäfer, A., Stark, R., & Vaitl, D. (2009). Long-term effects of cognitive behavior therapy on brain activation in spider phobia. *Psychiatry Research: Neuroimaging, 172,* 99–102. http://dx.doi.org/10.1016/j.pscychresns.2008.11.005

Schön, U. K., Denhov, A., & Topor, A. (2009). Social relationships as a decisive factor in recovering from severe mental illness. *International Journal of Social Psychiatry, 55,* 336–347.

Schore, A. N. (2012). *The science of the art of psychotherapy.* New York, NY: Norton.

Scull, A. (1989). *Social order/mental disorder.* Berkeley, CA: University of California Press.

Scull, A. (1993). *The most solitary of afflictions: Madness and society in Britain, 1700–1900.* New Haven, CT: Yale University Press.

Scull, A. (2005). *Madhouse: A tragic tale of megalomania and modern medicine.* New Haven, CT: Yale University Press.

Segal, H. (1980). *Melanie Klein.* New York, NY: Viking Press.

Shadish, W. R., Navarro, A. M., Matt, G. E., & Phillips, G. (2000). The effects of psychological therapies under clinically representative conditions: A meta-analysis. *Psychological Bulletin, 126,* 512–529. http://dx.doi.org/10.1037/0033-2909.126.4.512

Shapiro, D. A., & Shapiro, D. (1982). Meta-analysis of comparative therapy outcome studies: A replication and refinement. *Psychological Bulletin, 92,* 581–604. http://dx.doi.org/10.1037/0033-2909.92.3.581

Shorter, E. (1992). *From paralysis to fatigue: A history of psychosomatic illness in the modern era.* New York, NY: Free Press.

Shorter, E. (1993). *A short history of psychiatry.* New York, NY: Wiley.

Shorter, E. (1997). *A history of psychiatry: From the era of the asylum to the age of Prozac.* New York, NY: Wiley.

Shultz, S., & Dunbar, R. I. M. (2012). The social brain hypothesis: An evolutionary perspective on the neurobiology of social behavior. In S. D. Richmond, G. Rees, & S. J. L. Edwards (Eds.), *I know what you're thinking: Braining imaging and mental privacy* (pp. 13–28). Oxford, England: Oxford Scholarship. http://dx.doi.org/10.1093/acprof:oso/9780199596492.003.0002

Siegel, D. J. (2007). *The mindful brain: Reflection and attunement in the cultivation of well-being.* New York, NY: Norton.

Siegel, D. J. (2012). *The developing mind: How relationships and the brain interact to shape who we are* (2nd ed.). New York, NY: Guilford Press.

Simpson, J. A. (1990). Influence of attachment styles on romantic relationships. *Journal of Personality and Social Psychology, 59,* 971–980.

Smith, D. (1982). Trends in counseling and psychotherapy. *American Psychologist, 37,* 802–809. http://dx.doi.org/10.1037/0003-066X.37.7.802

Smith, M. L., & Glass, G. V. (1977). Meta-analysis of psychotherapy outcome studies. *American Psychologist, 32,* 752–760. http://dx.doi.org/10.1037/0003-066X.32.9.752

Smith, M. L., Glass, G. V., & Miller, T. I. (1980). *The benefits of psychotherapy.* Baltimore, MD: Johns Hopkins University Press.

Spitz, R. A. (1945). Hospitalism: An inquiry into the genesis of psychiatric conditions in early childhood. *The Psychoanalytic Study of the Child, 1,* 53–74.

Spitz, R. A. (1946a). Anaclitic depression: An inquiry into the genesis of psychiatric conditions in early childhood. *The Psychoanalytic Study of the Child, 2,* 313–342.

Spitz, R. A. (1946b). Hospitalism: A follow-up report. *The Psychoanalytic Study of the Child, 2,* 113–117.

Spock, B. (1946). *The common sense book of baby and child care.* New York, NY: Duell, Sloan, & Pearce.

Steering Committee. (2002). Empirically supported therapy relationships: Conclusions and recommendations of the Division 29 Task Force. In J. C. Norcross (Ed.), *Psychotherapy relationships that work* (pp. 441–443). Oxford, England: Oxford University Press.

Stewart, D. G., & Davis, K. L. (2008). The lobotomist. *The American Journal of Psychiatry, 165*, 457–458. http://dx.doi.org/10.1176/appi.ajp.2008.08020174

Stewart, K. A. (1992). *The York Retreat in light of the Quaker way.* York, England: Erbor Press.

Stiles, W. B., Barkham, M., Mellor-Clark, J., & Connell, J. (2008). Effectiveness of cognitive-behavioural, person-centred, and psychodynamic therapies in UK primary-care routine practice: Replication in a larger sample. *Psychological Medicine, 38*, 677–688. http://dx.doi.org/10.1017/S0033291707001511

Stiles, W. B., Barkham, M., Twigg, E., Mellor-Clark, J., & Cooper, M. (2006). Effectiveness of cognitive-behavioural, person-centred and psychodynamic therapies as practised in UK National Health Service settings. *Psychological Medicine, 36*, 555–566. http://dx.doi.org/10.1017/S0033291706007136

Stolorow, R., Brandchaft, B., & Atwood, G. (1987). *Psychoanalytic treatment: An intersubjective approach.* Hillsdale, NJ: Analytic Press.

Straube, T., Glauer, M., Dilger, S., Mentzel, H. J., & Miltner, W. H. (2006). Effects of cognitive-behavioral therapy on brain activation in specific phobia. *NeuroImage, 29*, 125–135. http://dx.doi.org/10.1016/j.neuroimage.2005.07.007

Strupp, H. H., & Hadley, S. W. (1979). Specific vs nonspecific factors in psychotherapy: A controlled study of outcome. *Archives of General Psychiatry, 36*, 1125–1136. http://dx.doi.org/10.1001/archpsyc.1979.01780100095009

Studd, J. (2006). Ovariotomy for menstrual madness and premenstrual syndrome—19th century history and lessons for current practice. *Gynecological Endocrinology, 22*, 411–415. http://dx.doi.org/10.1080/09513590600881503

Sullivan, R. (1996). The identity and work of the ancient Egyptian surgeon. *Journal of the Royal Society of Medicine, 89*, 467–473.

Summers, M. (1971). *The Malleus Maleficarum of Heinrich Kramer and James Sprenger.* Mineola, NY: Dover.

Swayze, V. W., II. (1995). Frontal leukotomy and related psychosurgical procedures in the era before antipsychotics (1935–1954): A historical overview. *The American Journal of Psychiatry, 152*, 505–515. http://dx.doi.org/10.1176/ajp.152.4.505

Teo, A. R., Choi, H., & Valenstein, M. (2013). Social relationships and depression: Ten-year follow-up from a nationally representative study. *PLoS ONE, 8*(4), e62396. http://dx.doi.org/10.1371/journal.pone. 0062396

Tew, J., Ramon, S., Slade, M., Bird, V., Melton, J., & Le Boutillier, C. (2012). Social factors and recovery from mental health difficulties: A review of the evidence. *British Journal of Social Work, 42,* 443–460. http://dx.doi.org/10.1093/bjsw/bcr076

Thiery, M. (1998). Battey's operation: An exercise in surgical frustration. *European Journal of Obstetrics, Gynecology, and Reproductive Biology, 81,* 243–246. http://dx.doi.org/10.1016/S0301-2115(98)00197-3

The top 10: The most influential therapists of the past quarter-century. (2007, March/April). *Psychotherapy Networker.* Retrieved from http://www.psychotherapynetworker.org

Trinke, S. J., & Bartholomew, K. (1997). Hierarchies of attachment relationships in young adulthood. *Journal of Social and Personal Relationships, 14,* 603–625. http://dx.doi.org/10.1177/0265407597145002

Tryon, W. W. (2014). *Cognitive neuroscience and psychotherapy: Network principles for a unified theory.* Waltham, MA: Academic Press.

Tsay, C. J. (2013). Julius Wagner-Jauregg and the legacy of malarial therapy for the treatment of general paresis of the insane. *The Yale Journal of Biology and Medicine, 86,* 245–254.

Tuke, S. (1996). *Description of the retreat: An institution near York, for insane persons of the Society of Friends.* London, England: Process Press. (Original work published 1813)

Uchino, B. N. (2006). Social support and health: A review of physiological processes potentially underlying links to disease outcomes. *Journal of Behavioral Medicine, 29,* 377–387. http://dx.doi.org/10.1007/s10865-006-9056-5

Umberson, D., & Montez, J. K. (2010). Social relationships and health: A flashpoint for health policy. *Journal of Health and Social Behavior, 51*(Suppl. 1), S54–S66. http://dx.doi.org/10.1177/0022146510383501

Unsworth, C. (1993). Law and lunacy in psychiatry's "golden age." *Oxford Journal of Legal Studies, 13,* 479–507. http://dx.doi.org/10.1093/ojls/13.4.479

Veith, I. (1965). *Hysteria: The history of a disease.* Chicago, IL: University of Chicago Press.

Viamontes, G. I., & Beitman, B. D. (2012). Neural substrates of psychotherapy. In R. D. Alarcon & J. B. Frank (Eds.), *The psychotherapy of hope: The legacy of persuasion and healing* (pp. 34–66). Baltimore, MD: Johns Hopkins University Press.

Waehler, C. A., Kalodner, C. R., Wampold, B. E., & Lichtenberg, J. W. (2000). Empirically supported treatments (ESTs) in perspective: Implications for counseling psychology training. *The Counseling Psychologist, 28,* 657–671. http://dx.doi.org/10.1177/0011000000285004

Wallin, D. J. (2007). *Attachment in psychotherapy.* New York, NY: Guilford Press.

Wampold, B. E. (2001a). *The great psychotherapy debate: Model, methods, and findings.* Mahwah, NJ: Erlbaum.

Wampold, B. E. (2001b). The psychotherapist. In J. C. Norcross, L. E. Beutler, & R. F. Levant (Eds.), *Evidence-based practices in mental health: Debate and dialogue on the fundamental questions* (pp. 200–207). Washington, DC: American Psychological Association.

Wampold, B. E. (2010). The research evidence for the common factors models: A historically situated perspective. In B. Duncan, S. Miller, B. Wampold, & M. Hubble (Eds.), *The heart and soul of change: Delivering what works in therapy* (2nd ed., pp. 49–81). Washington, DC: American Psychological Association. http://dx.doi.org/10.1037/12075-002

Wampold, B. E. (2012). Humanism as a common factor in psychotherapy. *Psychotherapy: Theory, Research, Practice, Training, 49,* 445–449. http://dx.doi.org/10.1037/a0027113

Wampold, B. E., & Brown, G. S. (2005). Estimating variability in outcomes attributable to therapists: A naturalistic study of outcomes in managed care. *Journal of Consulting and Clinical Psychology, 73,* 914–923. http://dx.doi.org/10.1037/0022-006X.73.5.914

Wampold, B. E., Mondin, G. W., Moody, M., Stich, F., Benson, K., & Ahn, H. (1997). A meta-analysis of outcome studies comparing bona fide psychotherapies: Empirically, "all must have prizes." *Psychological Bulletin, 122,* 203–215. http://dx.doi.org/10.1037/0033-2909.122.3.203

Wang, P. S., Lane, M., Olfson, M., Pincus, H. A., Wells, K. B., & Kessler, R. C. (2005). Twelve-month use of mental health services in the United States: Results from the National Comorbidity Survey Replication. *Archives of General Psychiatry, 62,* 629–640.

Wang, P. S., Demler, O., Olfson, M., Pincus, H. A., Wells, K. B., & Kessler, R. C. (2006). Changing profiles of service sectors used for mental health care in the United States. *The American Journal of Psychiatry, 163,* 1187–1198. http://dx.doi.org/10.1176/ajp.2006.163.7.1187

Warner, R. (2004). *Recovery from schizophrenia* (3rd ed.). New York, NY: Routledge.

Watson, J. B., & Watson, R. R. (1928). *Psychological care of the infant and child.* New York, NY: Norton.

Weiner, D. B. (1979). The apprenticeship of Philippe Pinel: A new document, "observations of Citizen Pussin on the insane." *The American Journal of Psychiatry, 136,* 1128–1134. http://dx.doi.org/10.1176/ajp.136.9.1128

Whitaker, R. (2002). *Mad in America.* Cambridge, MA: Perseus.

Whitaker, H. A., Stemmer, B., & Joanette, Y. (1996). A psychosurgical chapter in the history of cerebral localization: The six cases of Gottlieb Burkhardt. In C. Code, C. W. Wallesch, Y. Joanette, & A. Roch (Eds.), *Classic cases in neuropsychology* (pp. 275–304). New York, NY: Psychology Press.

Wilkinson, R., & Marmot, M. (Eds.). (2003). *Social determinants of health: The solid facts* (2nd ed.). Copenhagen, Denmark: World Health Organization.

Wright, M. (1996). William Emet Blatz. In G. A. Kimble, M. Wertheimer, & C. A. Boneau (Eds.), *Portraits of pioneers in psychology* (Vol. 2, pp. 199–212). Mahwah, NJ: Erlbaum.

Yalom, I. (1980). *Existential psychotherapy.* New York, NY: Basic Books.

Index

About the Author

David N. Elkins, PhD, is a professor emeritus of psychology in the Graduate School of Education and Psychology at Pepperdine University in Malibu, California, where he has trained clinical psychologists for nearly 30 years. As a licensed psychologist, Dr. Elkins has worked in hospital, community mental health, and private-practice settings. He is a fellow of the American Psychological Association (APA) and has served twice (1998–1999 and 2011–2012) as president of Division 32, Society for Humanistic Psychology, of APA. Dr. Elkins is the author of two previous books and a contributor to the current debate in clinical psychology regarding the determinants of effectiveness in psychotherapy. He has written numerous articles and given many professional presentations on the topic. *The Human Elements of Psychotherapy: A Nonmedical Model of Emotional Healing* is grounded in Dr. Elkins's experience as a clinician, professor, and author.